52-Week Bible Study Workbook for Black Women

A Yearlong Journey of Faith with Weekly Devotionals and Scripture Studies to Grow Closer to God

Welcome Aboard, Check Out This Limited-Time Free Bonus!

Ahoy, reader! Welcome to the Ahoy Publications family, and thanks for snagging a copy of this book! Since you've chosen to join us on this journey, we'd like to offer you something special.

Check out the link below for a FREE e-book filled with delightful facts about American History.

But that's not all - you'll also have access to our exclusive email list with even more free e-books and insider knowledge. Well, what are ye waiting for? Click the link below to join and set sail toward exciting adventures in American History.

Access your bonus here

https://ahoypublications.com/

Or, Scan the QR code!

Table of Contents

Dedication

To every woman opening these pages: May you discover profound clarity, walk in unshakeable confidence, and deepen your faith journey.

Introduction: Your Transformative Journey into God's Word

If you've ever desired to understand every book of Scripture, to feel truly confident in your grasp of God's Word, and to deepen your faith with unwavering clarity, you've come to the right place. This workbook is more than just a study guide; it's an invitation to a profound and personal encounter with the living God through His inspired text.

This guide is specifically for you, a woman of faith, guided by strength, grace, and an enduring spirit. This workbook is designed to meet you right where you are, offering perspectives and insights that resonate with your lived experience, illuminating how God's character and redemptive work are revealed in every part of His story. Here, you'll find a space where the ancient truths and profound wisdom of the Bible connect directly with your heart and circumstances, showing you more of who God is and how He works in the world.

Over the next 52 weeks, you'll discover a renewed sense of clarity, moving past confusion to grasp the core messages of each book. You'll build confidence, not just in what you know, but in your ability to interpret, apply, and share God's truth. Most importantly, you'll cultivate a deeper, more intimate faith, drawing closer to the Father, Son, and Holy Spirit with every turning page.

Each week of this yearlong journey will guide you through a specific book or section of the Bible. You'll find a devotional thought to set your heart, key scripture passages for focused reading, thoughtful questions designed to encourage personal reflection, and space to capture your insights and prayers. We'll move chronologically through the biblical narrative, ensuring you gain a holistic understanding of God's unfolding story.

To make the most of this workbook, we encourage you to:

- Set aside dedicated time: Even 15-20 minutes a few times a week can make a significant difference.

- Engage with the text: Read the suggested scriptures prayerfully.

- Be honest in your reflections: This is a safe space for growth.

- Pray always: Invite the Holy Spirit to be your ultimate teacher.

We are so glad you're here. Prepare to unlock the profound treasures within God's Word, to see God more clearly in His story, and to embark on a journey that will transform your understanding and deepen your walk with God like never before.

Part 1: The Foundation – The Pentateuch

Genesis, Exodus, Leviticus, Numbers, and Deuteronomy lay the essential groundwork for understanding God's relationship with humanity. They tell the story of creation, the fall, God's covenant with Abraham, the exodus from slavery in Egypt, the giving of the Law at Mount Sinai, and the preparations for entering the Promised Land.

As you work through these foundational texts, you'll uncover timeless truths about God's character, His promises, and His unwavering love for His people. You'll also explore themes of identity, liberation, obedience, and the importance of remembering God's faithfulness throughout your own journey.

Week 1: Genesis – The Beginning of All Things

Genesis, meaning "origins," is truly the book of beginnings. It's here that we encounter God as the ultimate Creator, speaking the universe and all of humanity into existence with intentionality and profound love. We witness the creation of the first man and woman, the introduction of sin and its devastating consequences, and God's earliest covenants, including the pivotal promise to Abraham. This promise to make him into a great nation and bless all peoples through him lays the indispensable groundwork for the nation of Israel and, ultimately, for the coming of the Messiah. This week, we'll reflect on our own origins as uniquely crafted beings in God's image, His limitless creative power, and the enduring impact of both our choices and His unwavering faithfulness.

Devotional Thought: Created with Purpose

Take a moment to simply be. Look around you, whether at the grandeur of nature or the intricate details of a simple object, and consider the miracle of creation. The Bible opens with a powerful declaration: "In the beginning, God created..." (Genesis 1:1). It's a profound truth about your existence. You were not an accident.

You were designed, woven together by a masterful Creator who thought of you before the foundations of the world. Genesis reminds us our true identity is rooted in divine design. Humanity, both male and female, is made in God's image, carrying His essence, His creativity, and His purpose. God uniquely fashioned women with divine wisdom, creating them as powerful and complementary partners. This distinct design reflects His glory in an essential way, contributing to His grand purpose. Let that profound truth settle deep within your spirit this week.

How does knowing you are intentionally created by God for His good purpose transform your perspective on yourself, your challenges, and your future?

Key Scriptures:

- **Genesis 1:1-31:** The Creation Account
- **Genesis 2:7:** The Breath of Life
- **Genesis 1:26-28:** Created in God's Image
- **Genesis 3:1-19:** The Fall of Humanity
- **Genesis 12:1-3:** God's Covenant with Abraham

Reflection Questions:

1. As you read Genesis 1, what new insights or feelings emerge about God's power and meticulous nature as the Creator?

2. Considering the early chapters of Genesis reveal God's foundational design for humanity, how does this comprehensive understanding of divine creation deepen your grasp of God's purpose for human life, and specifically for your identity, worth, and role as a woman of faith?

3. Genesis 3 describes the entry of sin into the world. How do you see the consequences of that first act of disobedience still impacting humanity and your own life today?

4. God's foundational promise to Abraham in Genesis 12:1-3 centered on establishing a great nation and extending blessing through his lineage. How does this divine initiation of God's covenant plan reveal His steadfast character, and what does Abraham's obedient faith teach you about walking with God?

5. What is one specific way you can live out your divine design this week, acknowledging God as your Creator and the source of your existence?

Week 1 Workbook

Date: _____

Key Takeaways from Devotional Thought:

_____

_____

_____

_____

_____

Insights from Genesis:

_____

_____

_____

_____

Devotional Reflection: What Biblical truth or principle from this week's study stood out to me?

_____

_____

_____

_____

_____

_____

_____

_____

_____

Week 2: Exodus – Liberation and Covenant

Exodus, meaning "exit" or "departure," chronicles one of the most pivotal events in biblical history: the miraculous liberation of the Israelite people from brutal slavery in Egypt.

This book reveals God's profound power as He confronts the oppressive might of Pharaoh through a series of awe-inspiring plagues, culminating in the parting of the Red Sea. Beyond the dramatic escape, Exodus also details the giving of the Ten Commandments and the establishment of the covenant at Mount Sinai, where God formalizes His relationship with Israel, providing laws and instructions for worship and holy living.

This week, we will explore themes of divine deliverance, the nature of true freedom, and the profound significance of God's covenant promises to His people: promises that still resonate deeply in our lives today.

Devotional Thought: God Hears Your Cry

The Israelites had endured generations of enslavement, their cries echoing under the weight of oppression. But Exodus opens with a powerful truth: "The Israelites groaned in their slavery and cried out, and their cry for help went up to God" (Exodus 2:23). God heard them. He saw their suffering, and He acted. In our own lives, there are moments, seasons, or even long periods where we might feel trapped, burdened, or unseen.

The narrative of Exodus serves as a potent reminder that God is not distant from your struggles. He is a God who hears, who sees, and who intervenes. This week, reflect on any areas in your life where you long for liberation or feel overwhelmed. How does the story of the Exodus affirm God's attentive ear and His power to deliver you?

Key Scriptures:

- **Exodus 2:23-25:** God Hears His People's Groaning
- **Exodus 3:7-10:** God Calls Moses and Promises Deliverance
- **Exodus 7-12:** The Ten Plagues
- **Exodus 14:** The Parting of the Red Sea
- **Exodus 20:1-17:** The Ten Commandments

Reflection Questions:

1. What does the story of God calling Moses at the burning bush (Exodus 3) reveal about God's character and His approach to choosing leaders?

2. The Ten Plagues were God's judgment on Egypt and its gods. What do these events teach you about God's sovereignty and His opposition to injustice?

3. How does the miraculous crossing of the Red Sea (Exodus 14) speak to God's power to make a way where there seems to be no way in your own life?

4. The Ten Commandments (Exodus 20) are the foundation of God's law. Which commandment resonates most with you this week, and how can you apply it more intentionally?

5. Reflect on a time when you experienced God's deliverance or felt Him hear your cry. How does that personal experience connect with the grand narrative of the Exodus?

Week 2 Workbook

Date: _____

Key Takeaways from Devotional Thought:

_____

_____

_____

_____

_____

Insights from Exodus:

_____

_____

_____

_____

_____

Devotional Reflection: What Biblical insights did I gain about leadership this week?

_____

_____

_____

_____

_____

_____

_____

_____

_____

_____

Week 3: Leviticus – Holiness and Worship

Leviticus, often perceived as a challenging book due to its detailed laws and rituals, is in fact a profound revelation of God's holiness and His desire for His people to live in consecrated relationship with Him. Named after the Levites, the priestly tribe, this book outlines the sacrificial system, the functions of the priesthood, and numerous regulations concerning purity, worship, and ethical conduct. It teaches Israel how to approach a holy God and how to live as a set-apart nation in His presence.

This week, we will uncover the timeless principles embedded in these ancient texts: principles that illuminate God's character, our need for atonement, and the call to live a life of holiness that reflects His divine nature.

Devotional Thought: Set Apart for His Purpose

Leviticus repeatedly echoes the command: "Be holy, because I am holy" (Leviticus 11:44-45).

In a world that often pressures us to conform, the call to holiness can feel counter-cultural, even isolating. Remember this: true holiness is not about rigid legalism or self-righteousness; it is about being set apart for God's divine purpose. It's about reflecting His character in our thoughts, words, and actions, not out of obligation, but out of a deep love for Him and a desire to honor His presence in our lives.

Embracing holiness can be a powerful act of self-love and spiritual resilience, affirming our sacred worth and agency in a world that too often seeks to define us by its own standards. When we intentionally choose to live a life consecrated to God, we become powerful witnesses to His transforming grace and an embodiment of His light.

Key Scriptures:

- **Leviticus 1:1-9:** The Purpose of Offerings
- **Leviticus 11:44-45:** The Command to Be Holy
- **Leviticus 16:** The Day of Atonement (Yom Kippur)
- **Leviticus 17:11:** The Significance of Blood for Atonement
- **Leviticus 19:1-2, 18:** Holiness, Justice, and Love for Neighbor

Reflection Questions:

1. Leviticus details a complex system of sacrifices. What do these rituals teach you about the seriousness of sin and God's provision for atonement, even before Christ?

2. The repeated command "Be holy, because I am holy" is central to God's character and our calling. How does God's holiness transform and guide your daily conduct, beyond religious observances?

3. The Day of Atonement (Leviticus 16) was a crucial annual event. How does understanding this ritual deepen your appreciation for Jesus Christ as the ultimate sacrifice for your sins (Hebrews 9:11-14)?

4. Leviticus 19:18 commands, "Love your neighbor as yourself." How does this command, found within a book of laws, demonstrate the relational heart of God's holiness?

5. What is one practical step you can take this week to intentionally set yourself apart for God's purposes, reflecting His holiness in your sphere of influence?

Week 3 Workbook

Date: _____

Key Takeaways from Devotional Thought:

_____

_____

_____

_____

_____

Insights from Leviticus:

_____

_____

_____

_____

_____

Devotional Reflection: What Biblical truths about living with purpose did you learn from God's Word this week?

_____

_____

_____

_____

_____

_____

_____

_____

_____

Week 4: Numbers – Wilderness Wanderings and God's Faithfulness

Numbers, the fourth book of the Pentateuch, takes its name from the two censuses of the Israelite people documented within its pages. More profoundly, it chronicles the approximately 40 years of Israel's wilderness wanderings, a period marked by both divine guidance and human rebellion. Following their liberation from Egypt and the giving of the Law at Sinai, the Israelites faced numerous challenges: distrust in God's provision, complaints, and outright disobedience, which led to consequences for an entire generation.

Amidst their failures, God's faithfulness shines through His constant presence, His miraculous provision of manna and water, and His enduring patience. This week, we will journey with Israel through the wilderness, reflecting on the lessons of faith, consequences of doubt, and the unwavering steadfastness of God's character, even when His people falter.

Devotional Thought: When the Journey Gets Long

The wilderness journey in Numbers is a powerful metaphor for our own lives. There are seasons when the path feels long, provisions seem scarce, and the destination appears distant. The Israelites, despite witnessing incredible miracles, often succumbed to grumbling, fear, and a desire to return to what was familiar, even if it was bondage. Their story serves as a stark reminder that physical freedom does not automatically equate to spiritual freedom. True liberation requires a heart that trusts God, even when the way is unclear.

We often navigate complex and prolonged journeys where resilience is tested. How do we respond when the wilderness feels endless? This week, let the book of Numbers encourage you that even in times of wandering, God remains present, providing, and patiently guiding you toward your promised land. His faithfulness is not dependent on your perfection, but on His unchanging nature.

Key Scriptures:

- **Numbers 13:1-3, 26-33:** The Spies Sent to Canaan and Their Report

- **Numbers 14:1-12, 26-35:** The People's Rebellion and God's Judgment

- **Numbers 20:2-13:** Water from the Rock (and Moses' disobedience)

- **Numbers 21:4-9:** The Bronze Snake (God's provision for healing)

- **Numbers 23:19:** God Is Not a Man That He Should Lie

Reflection Questions:

1. The Israelites' fear and unbelief after the spies' report (Numbers 13-14) led to severe consequences. How does fear of the unknown or doubt in God's promises sometimes prevent you from moving forward in your own faith journey?

2. Despite Israel's repeated complaints and rebellion, God continued to provide for them (manna, water). What does this reveal about God's enduring patience and grace?

3. Moses, a mighty leader, was disciplined for his disobedience (Numbers 20). What does this teach us about accountability and the importance of revering God's commands, regardless of our position?

4. The story of the bronze snake (Numbers 21:4-9) foreshadows salvation through Christ. What parallels do you see between looking to the snake for physical healing and looking to Jesus for spiritual healing?

5. Consider a challenging period in your life. How did God's faithfulness become evident during that time, even if you only recognized it in retrospect??

Week 4 Workbook

Date: _____

Key Takeaways from Devotional Thought:

_____

_____

_____

_____

_____

Insights from Numbers:

_____

_____

_____

_____

Devotional Reflection: What Biblical insights on faith did you gain from God's Word this week?

_____

_____

_____

_____

_____

_____

_____

_____

_____

Week 5: Deuteronomy – Remember and Recommit

Deuteronomy, the fifth and final book of the Pentateuch, means "second law." It's not a new law, but rather a powerful restatement and exposition of the Law given at Mount Sinai, delivered by Moses to the new generation of Israelites on the plains of Moab, just before they entered the Promised Land. This book serves as a vital bridge between the wilderness wanderings and the settlement in Canaan.

Through a series of impassioned speeches, Moses reminds the people of God's faithfulness throughout their history, reiterates their covenant responsibilities, and urges them to remember, obey, and love God with all their heart, soul, and might.

This week, we will delve into Moses' final appeals, understanding the critical importance of remembering God's past mercies and recommitting our lives to His commands, preparing our hearts for the "promised lands" He leads us into.

Devotional Thought: The Power of Remembering

"Remember how the Lord your God led you all the way in the wilderness these forty years, to humble and test you in order to know what was in your heart, whether or not you would keep his commands" (Deuteronomy 8:2). Moses, standing on the brink of the Promised Land, knew that a new generation could easily forget the hardships and the miracles that brought them there.

He repeatedly calls them to *remember*. In our own lives, remembering is a powerful act. Remembering God's past faithfulness, His past deliverances, and His unwavering presence through trials gives us strength for what lies ahead.

It counters the narratives of scarcity, fear, and forgetfulness that the world often imposes. This week, let's intentionally pause and recall the specific moments, big or small, where God showed up for you. How does remembering His past faithfulness empower you to trust Him with your present and future?

Key Scriptures:

- **Deuteronomy 6:4-9:** The Shema – Love the Lord Your God

- **Deuteronomy 8:2-3, 11-18:** Remembering God's Provision and Warning Against Forgetfulness

- **Deuteronomy 10:12-13:** What God Requires

- **Deuteronomy 28:1-14:** Blessings for Obedience

- **Deuteronomy 30:19-20:** Choose Life

Reflection Questions:

1. Moses emphasizes the importance of *remembering* God's acts in the wilderness. What are some significant ways God has led, provided for, or disciplined you in your "wilderness seasons"?

2. The "Shema" (Deuteronomy 6:4-9) commands absolute love and devotion to God. How do you practically demonstrate your love for God with all your heart, soul, and strength in your daily life?

3. Deuteronomy presents blessings for obedience and consequences for disobedience. How does understanding these principles motivate you to align your life more fully with God's will?

4. Moses presents the Israelites with a choice: life or death, blessings or curses (Deuteronomy 30:19-20). What "choices" are you facing today, and how can you intentionally "choose life" by choosing God's way?

5. As you conclude your study of the Pentateuch, what is the most significant truth or principle you've learned about God's character and His relationship with humanity that you want to carry forward?

Week 5 Workbook

Date: _____

Key Takeaways from Devotional Thought:

_____

_____

_____

_____

_____

Insights from Deuteronomy:

_____

_____

_____

_____

_____

Devotional Reflection: How did this week's study deepen your understanding of God's will for your life?

_____

_____

_____

_____

_____

_____

_____

_____

_____

Part 2: God's People and Their History

Having laid the foundational truths of creation, covenant, liberation, and law in the Pentateuch, we now turn the page to witness these divine principles unfold in the life of a nation. Part 2 of our journey, "God's People and Their History," moves beyond the wilderness and into the Promised Land, chronicling the triumphs and trials of Israel as they navigate their identity as a people set apart for God.

This section will delve into the historical books of the Old Testament, beginning with the conquest of Canaan under Joshua and continuing through the eras of the Judges, the

establishment of the monarchy with kings like Saul, David, and Solomon, and ultimately, the tragic division of the kingdom.

We will observe the intricate dance between divine faithfulness and human fallibility, the consequences of both obedience and rebellion, and the persistent presence of God working through imperfect people in complex circumstances.

Week 6: Joshua – Conquering and Settling

Joshua, the sixth book of the Old Testament, marks a significant transition in Israel's history. No longer wandering in the wilderness, the Israelites, under the new leadership of **Joshua**, Moses' successor, are now poised to enter and conquer the **Promised Land** of Canaan.

This book is a powerful narrative of faith, courage, and divine fulfillment, detailing the military campaigns to claim the land God had promised to Abraham, Isaac, and Jacob. It showcases God's faithfulness in delivering on His promises and His power in overcoming formidable obstacles. Beyond the battles, Joshua also records the division of the land among the twelve tribes, establishing Israel as a settled nation.

This week, we'll explore themes of leadership, the nature of spiritual warfare, the importance of obedience in securing God's promises, and the ultimate triumph of God's plan, even in the face of immense challenges.

Devotional Thought: Stepping into Your Promised Land

After forty years of wilderness wandering, a new generation stands at the threshold of the Promised Land, ready to face giants and fortified cities. Their journey into Canaan, led by Joshua, mirrors our own calls to step into the "promised lands" God has for us, whether it's a new opportunity, overcoming a long-standing challenge, or fulfilling a divine purpose. Just as Israel needed to confront and conquer, we too will face obstacles. But the book of Joshua reminds us that the victory belongs to God. He promised to be with Joshua, just as He promises to be with us: "I will be with you; I will never leave you nor forsake you" (Joshua 1:5).

This week, reflect on the "Canaan" in your own life: the next step, the breakthrough, the calling God is inviting you into. What giants do you need to face, and how will you lean on God's presence and power to conquer?

Key Scriptures:

- **Joshua 1:6-9:** God's Charge to Joshua – Be Strong and Courageous
- **Joshua 3:14-17:** Crossing the Jordan River
- **Joshua 6:1-20:** The Fall of Jericho
- **Joshua 10:12-14:** The Day the Sun Stood Still
- **Joshua 24:14-15:** Joshua's Final Charge – Choose Whom You Will Serve

Reflection Questions:

1. In Joshua 1:6-9, God repeatedly tells Joshua to "be strong and courageous." What specific fears or uncertainties do you need God's strength and courage to face right now?

2. The miraculous crossing of the Jordan (Joshua 3) highlights God's power to clear paths. Where do you need God to make a way for you today, even if it seems impossible?

3. The battle of Jericho (Joshua 6) was won through unconventional obedience. What situation in your life requires you to trust God's unusual strategy rather than your own logic or strength?

4. Joshua's leadership was marked by unwavering faith and consistent obedience. What qualities of his leadership can you seek to emulate in your own areas of influence?

5. Joshua's final challenge in Joshua 24:15 is to choose to serve the Lord. What does it mean for you, personally, to make that deliberate choice daily?

Week 6 Workbook

Date: _____

Key Takeaways from Devotional Thought:

_____

_____

_____

_____

_____

Insights from Joshua:

_____

_____

_____

_____

_____

Devotional Reflection: How did this week's study of God's Word shape your understanding of His miraculous power in your life?

_____

_____

_____

_____

_____

_____

_____

_____

_____

_____

Week 7: Judges – Cycles of Disobedience and Deliverance

The book of Judges plunges us into a turbulent and often unsettling period of Israel's history, immediately following Joshua's death. Without a central human leader, and before the establishment of a monarchy, Israel falls into a destructive cycle: they abandon God, are oppressed by surrounding nations, cry out to God for help, and God raises a "judge" to deliver them. Once delivered, they eventually relapse into idolatry and disobedience, restarting the cycle.

This book highlights the profound consequences of spiritual apostasy and the desperate need for righteous leadership. Even in this era of chaos and moral decline, God's enduring patience and unwavering commitment to His covenant with Israel shine through.

This week, we will explore these recurring patterns, recognizing humanity's propensity for rebellion and God's persistent grace in delivering His people, ultimately pointing to Israel's desperate need for a true king.

Devotional Thought: Breaking the Cycle

"In those days Israel had no king; everyone did as they saw fit" (Judges 21:25). This phrase, repeated like a mournful refrain throughout Judges, encapsulates the core problem of the era: a lack of central authority and, more importantly, a lack of spiritual compass. The Israelites were caught in a repetitive cycle of sin, suffering, repentance, and deliverance. It's a powerful mirror to our own lives. How often do we find ourselves repeating patterns of behavior or thought that lead us away from God's best for us?

Judges reminds us that true freedom isn't just about escaping oppression, but about breaking free from the spiritual patterns that bind us. This week, identify a cycle in your life, such as a recurring negative thought, a habit, or a response, that you want to break. How can you, like the Israelites eventually needed a king, surrender more fully to the sovereignty of Christ as your ultimate King to find lasting deliverance and break free?

Key Scriptures:

- **Judges 2:11-19:** The Cycle of Apostasy, Oppression, and Deliverance

- **Judges 4:4-9:** Deborah – A Woman of Courage and Leadership

- **Judges 6:11-16:** Gideon's Call – From Weakness to God's Strength

- **Judges 16:1-21:** Samson – Strength, Weakness, and Consequences

- **Judges 21:25:** The Recurring Theme – No King in Israel

Reflection Questions:

1. The cycle of sin and deliverance is prominent in Judges. Can you identify a similar cycle in your own life that you are currently navigating or seeking to break?

2. Deborah (Judges 4) was a judge and prophetess who led Israel to victory. What does her story teach you about God's ability to use women in powerful leadership roles, even in challenging times?

3. Gideon (Judges 6-7) initially doubted God's call but ultimately led with divine power. Where do you need to overcome doubt and step out in faith, trusting God's extraordinary strength for your ordinary circumstances?

4. Samson's story (Judges 13-16) is a tragic narrative of gifts misused and potential squandered. What lessons can you draw from his life about the importance of spiritual discipline and resisting temptation?

5. The book of Judges ends with the statement, "everyone did as they saw fit." How does this highlight the importance of not relying on personal feelings or cultural norms, but on God's unchanging truth as our guide?

Week 7 Workbook

Date: _____

Key Takeaways from Devotional Thought:

_____

_____

_____

_____

_____

Insights from Judges:

_____

_____

_____

_____

_____

Devotional Reflection: What truth about spiritual discipline from the Scriptures stood out to you this week?

_____

_____

_____

_____

_____

_____

_____

_____

_____

_____

Week 8: Ruth –
Loyalty, Love, and Redemption

Following the tumultuous era of the Judges, the book of Ruth offers a refreshing and intimate glimpse into the lives of ordinary people demonstrating extraordinary faith and faithfulness. Set during the period of the Judges, this short but profound narrative centers on **Ruth**, a Moabite woman, who, after the death of her husband, chooses unwavering loyalty to her Israelite mother-in-law, Naomi, and to the God of Israel. Her story is one of profound devotion, hard work, and ultimately, **redemption**, as she finds a kinsman-redeemer in Boaz.

Ruth's narrative beautifully illustrates themes of radical commitment, divine providence in the mundane, and the expansive nature of God's grace, extending even to those outside of Israel.

This week, we'll explore how God works through loyal relationships and seemingly small acts of kindness to weave together a greater story of hope and provide a vital link in the lineage of King David and, ultimately, Jesus Christ.

Devotional Thought: Cultivating Unwavering Loyalty

"Where you go I will go, and where you stay I will stay. Your people will be my people and your God my God" (Ruth 1:16). These iconic words spoken by Ruth to Naomi are a powerful testament to **unwavering loyalty**; a quality that often feels rare in a world that promotes individualism and transient connections. Ruth's commitment wasn't born out of convenience but out of deep love and a radical decision to embrace a new people and a new God, even in the face of hardship and uncertainty.

Ruth's narrative affirms the profound impact of faithful devotion. It reminds us that our commitment, whether to family, friends, or our spiritual walk, can be a potent force for good and a conduit for God's redemptive work. This week, reflect on the relationships and commitments in your life. Where is God calling you to embody Ruth-like loyalty, trusting that even seemingly small acts of faithfulness can yield immense blessings and contribute to His grand design?

Key Scriptures:

- **Ruth 1:16-18:** Ruth's Vow of Loyalty to Naomi
- **Ruth 2:8-12:** Boaz's Kindness to Ruth
- **Ruth 3:9-11:** Ruth's Appeal to Boaz as Kinsman-Redeemer
- **Ruth 4:9-17:** The Redemption and Birth of Obed
- **Proverbs 31:10:** A Woman of Noble Character (often associated with Ruth)

Reflection Questions:

1. Ruth's decision to stay with Naomi demonstrates extraordinary loyalty. How have you experienced or witnessed profound loyalty in your own life, and what impact did it have?

2. Boaz's treatment of Ruth goes beyond legal obligation, showcasing grace and compassion. How can you extend kindness and grace to others in your sphere of influence, especially to those who might be overlooked?

3. The concept of the **kinsman-redeemer** (Boaz) is central to Ruth's story and foreshadows Christ. How does understanding Boaz's role deepen your appreciation for Jesus as your ultimate Redeemer?

4. Ruth's story highlights divine providence God working behind the scenes in seemingly ordinary events. Can you recall a time in your life when you recognized God's hand at work in circumstances that initially seemed insignificant?

5. What is one area of your life where God is calling you to show greater **faithfulness** or **loyalty**, even when it requires sacrifice or inconvenience?

Week 8 Workbook

Date: _____

Key Takeaways from Devotional Thought:

_____

_____

_____

_____

_____

Insights from Ruth:

_____

_____

_____

_____

_____

Devotional Reflection: What Biblical insights on trusting God's plan, especially in tough situations, did you gain this week?

_____

_____

_____

_____

_____

_____

_____

_____

_____

Week 9: 1 & 2 Samuel – From Judges to Kings, The Davidic Dynasty

The books of 1 and 2 Samuel collectively bridge the gap between the chaotic era of the Judges and the establishment of Israel's monarchy, culminating in the reign of its greatest king, David. **1 Samuel** introduces us to **Samuel**, the last judge and a pivotal prophet who anoints Israel's first king, **Saul**. Though chosen for his imposing presence, Saul's reign is marked by disobedience and a tragic decline. God then raises up **David**, a humble shepherd, chosen not for his outward appearance but for his heart. **2 Samuel** chronicles David's ascent to the throne over all Israel, his military triumphs, his establishment of Jerusalem as the capital, and God's unconditional covenant with him, promising an eternal dynasty.

However, the narrative also honestly depicts David's profound moral failures (such as his sin with Bathsheba) and the devastating consequences that ripple through his family and kingdom. Together, these books explore themes of leadership, obedience, the nature of true worship, the weight of sin, the power of repentance, and God's unwavering faithfulness even in the midst of human brokenness.

This week, we will examine the complex journey of Israel's first kings and the enduring legacy of David.

Devotional Thought: Flawed Leaders, Faithful God, and the Posture of the Heart

"The Lord does not look at the things people look at. People look at the outward appearance, but the Lord looks at the heart" (1 Samuel 16:7). This foundational truth, revealed when David is chosen, sets the stage for the dramatic contrast between Saul and David. Saul, impressive outwardly, loses God's favor due to a disobedient heart.

David, though a "man after God's own heart" (Acts 13:22), commits grievous sins, but his readiness to repent and his deep devotion lead to restoration. These books remind us that God's assessment of us goes beyond superficial traits to the true condition of our hearts.

The stories of Saul and David offer both inspiration and caution. They affirm that God sees and chooses the overlooked, but also highlight the profound importance of humility, obedience, and a repentant spirit, especially when entrusted with influence. This week, reflect on the posture of your own heart. Are you cultivating a heart that truly seeks God's will, is quick to repent, and trusts His power to lead, even through your imperfections?

Key Scriptures:

- **1 Samuel 1:27-28:** Hannah's Prayer and Dedication of Samuel
- **1 Samuel 8:4-7:** Israel's Demand for a King
- **1 Samuel 13:13-14:** Saul's Disobedience and Rejection
- **1 Samuel 16:7:** God Looks at the Heart
- **1 Samuel 17:45-47:** David and Goliath
- **2 Samuel 5:1-5:** David Becomes King Over All Israel
- **2 Samuel 7:8-16:** God's Covenant with David (Eternal Dynasty)
- **2 Samuel 11:1-5, 14-17:** David's Sin with Bathsheba and Uriah
- **2 Samuel 12:1-13:** Nathan Confronts David; David's Repentance

Reflection Questions:

1. How does Israel's demand for a king (1 Samuel 8), rather than continuing to trust God as their ruler, parallel any areas in your life where you might be tempted to rely on human systems over divine guidance?

2. The contrast between Saul and David highlights the importance of a leader's heart. What qualities of heart does God value most in those He uses, and how can you cultivate these in your own life?

3. God's covenant with David in 2 Samuel 7 is foundational to biblical prophecy. How does understanding this promise deepen your appreciation for Jesus as the ultimate descendant of David and King of Kings?

4. David's serious sin with Bathsheba and Uriah, followed by his profound repentance, offers powerful lessons. What does his response teach you about addressing your own failures and seeking God's forgiveness?

5. Despite immense challenges and personal failures, David remained a man after God's own heart. What does this teach you about God's grace and His ability to work through imperfect people to accomplish His perfect will?

Week 9 Workbook

Date: _____

Key Takeaways from Devotional Thought:

_____

_____

_____

_____

_____

Insights from 1&2 Samuel:

_____

_____

_____

_____

_____

Devotional Reflection: How did this week's study deepen your understanding of God's perspective on asking for forgiveness?

_____

_____

_____

_____

_____

_____

_____

_____

_____

_____

Week 10: 1 & 2 Kings – The Rise and Fall of Kingdoms

The books of 1 and 2 Kings continue the historical narrative of Israel, picking up immediately after the close of 2 Samuel with the end of King David's reign and the beginning of his son Solomon's. These books chronicle the united kingdom's golden age under Solomon, marked by the building of the Temple, but quickly pivot to the tragic **division of the kingdom** into Israel (north) and Judah (south) after Solomon's death.

They then follow the tumultuous reigns of a long succession of kings, detailing their obedience or disobedience to God, their alliances, wars, and the ministries of powerful prophets like Elijah and Elisha who challenged the prevailing idolatry. Ultimately, 1 and 2 Kings provide a sobering account of both kingdoms' eventual decline and their respective exiles, Israel to Assyria and Judah to Babylon, due to their persistent turning away from God.

This week, we will examine the patterns of leadership, the consequences of national sin, the unwavering voices of God's prophets, and the unfolding of God's justice and mercy in the rise and fall of kingdoms.

Devotional Thought: Leadership, Legacy, and Lasting Consequences

The books of Kings offer a profound study in **leadership and legacy**. We see kings who begin well, like Solomon, but then stray; and kings who are wholly devoted to idolatry, leading their people astray. Their choices, whether good or bad, had ripple effects that impacted generations. The recurring theme is that a nation's destiny was often tied to the spiritual health of its leader. For women who often find themselves in leadership roles, whether formally in careers, informally in families, or powerfully in their communities, these narratives are particularly relevant. They challenge us to consider the legacy we are building, not just for ourselves, but for those who follow. Are our choices rooted in God's wisdom, or are we swayed by worldly desires or pressures?

This week, reflect on the leaders in 1 and 2 Kings. What kind of legacy are you striving to build through your leadership and influence, and how are you ensuring it's one that honors God and blesses future generations?

Key Scriptures:

- **1 Kings 3:5-14:** Solomon Asks for Wisdom
- **1 Kings 11:1-13:** Solomon's Idolatry and Its Consequences
- **1 Kings 18:20-39:** Elijah and the Prophets of Baal on Mount Carmel
- **2 Kings 17:7-18:** Israel's Rebellion and Exile
- **2 Kings 25:1-12:** Judah's Fall and Exile to Babylon
- **Proverbs 14:34:** Righteousness Exalts a Nation

Reflection Questions:

1. Solomon was granted immense wisdom by God but eventually succumbed to idolatry. What does his story teach us about the importance of continued vigilance and faithfulness, even after great blessings?

2. The division of the kingdom marks a tragic turning point. What lessons can be learned from the choices that led to this division, both from the leaders and the people?

3. Prophets like Elijah and Elisha often stood alone against corrupt kings and widespread idolatry. What does their courage teach you about standing firm in your faith, even when it's unpopular or challenging?

4. Both Israel and Judah ultimately went into exile due to their disobedience. How do these accounts underscore the principle that there are consequences for persistent turning away from God?

5. Despite the repeated failures of the kings and the people, God's promise to David's line (2 Samuel 7) remained. How does God's enduring faithfulness, even in judgment, bring you hope today?

Week 10 Workbook

Date: _____

Key Takeaways from Devotional Thought:

_____

_____

_____

_____

_____

Insights from 1 & 2 Kings:

_____

_____

_____

_____

_____

Devotional Reflection: How did this week's study deepen your understanding of God's call to holiness in your life?

_____

_____

_____

_____

_____

_____

_____

_____

_____

Week 11: 1 & 2 Chronicles – A Retelling for Renewal

The books of 1 and 2 Chronicles largely cover the same historical ground as 2 Samuel and 1 & 2 Kings, but they do so from a different perspective and with a distinct purpose. Written after the return of the exiles from Babylon, Chronicles aims to encourage and instruct a disheartened nation struggling to rebuild. Rather than focusing on the northern kingdom of Israel, Chronicles centers almost exclusively on the **southern kingdom of Judah** and the **Davidic line**, emphasizing the importance of the **Temple, the priesthood, and proper worship**.

It highlights good kings who were devoted to God and whose reforms brought revival, while often glossing over the flaws of figures like David and Solomon to present them as ideals. The Chronicler's message is clear: God is faithful to His covenant, and the path to national restoration lies in faithfulness, repentance, and a renewed commitment to worship.

This week, we will explore this unique retelling of Israel's history, discerning its emphasis on God's enduring covenant, the centrality of worship, and the hope of restoration for a people who return to Him.

Devotional Thought: Reclaiming Your Narrative

Imagine rebuilding after great loss, your home, your community, your very identity. That was the context for the original audience of Chronicles. They needed to remember who they were as God's people, and why their history mattered. The Chronicler didn't just list facts; he curated their story to emphasize God's faithfulness, the power of repentance, and the critical role of worship.

The act of **reclaiming and retelling our narratives** is incredibly powerful. Our stories, like Judah's, are often complex, marked by both profound suffering and incredible resilience. Chronicles invites us to look at our past through a lens of God's overarching purpose, finding meaning and hope even in challenging chapters. It reminds us that setbacks are not the final word and that a renewed focus on worship and covenant with God can be the key to our own restoration and future flourishing. This week, consider your personal or communal narrative. How can you view your history through the lens of God's faithfulness, recognizing His hand at work, and allowing it to fuel your hope and worship for the future?

Key Scriptures:

- **1 Chronicles 17:11-14:** Reiteration of the Davidic Covenant
- **2 Chronicles 7:14:** God's Promise of Healing and Restoration
- **2 Chronicles 16:9:** The Lord's Eyes Search the Whole Earth
- **2 Chronicles 20:1-30:** Jehoshaphat's Prayer and God's Deliverance in Worship
- **2 Chronicles 33:10-13:** Manasseh's Repentance and Restoration
- **2 Chronicles 36:15-21:** The Final Judgment and Exile

Reflection Questions:

1. Chronicles emphasizes the importance of the Davidic covenant and the Temple. How does understanding the centrality of worship and God's presence shape your own spiritual practices today?

2. The Chronicler highlights kings who sought the Lord and brought about spiritual reform. What characteristics did these "good" kings exhibit, and how can you apply them to your own life and spheres of influence?

3. The book of 2 Chronicles 7:14 is a powerful promise of healing for a repentant nation. How does this verse speak to the potential for healing and restoration in your own life or community when there is genuine repentance and turning to God?

4. Jehoshaphat's victory in 2 Chronicles 20 came through worship and trust, not military might. What situation are you facing where you need to trust God's unconventional methods and lean into worship as your strategy?

5. Despite repeated cycles of unfaithfulness, Chronicles consistently points to God's enduring patience and desire for His people's return. How does this constant theme of divine grace encourage you in your walk with God?

Week 11 Workbook

Date: _____

Key Takeaways from Devotional Thought:

_____
_____
_____
_____
_____

Insights from 1&2 Chronicles:

_____
_____
_____
_____
_____

Devotional Reflection: What truth from God's Word about standing firm in faith became clearer to you this week?

_____
_____
_____
_____
_____
_____
_____
_____
_____
_____

Week 12: Ezra & Nehemiah – Return, Rebuilding, and Revival

The books of Ezra and Nehemiah present a powerful two-part narrative of the post-exilic period, detailing the remarkable return of the Jewish exiles to Jerusalem and their monumental efforts to rebuild their homeland, both physically and spiritually. **Ezra**, a priest and scribe, leads a wave of returnees focused on **reconstructing the Temple** and, critically, **restoring God's Law** among the people. His passion for the Word and call to repentance lead to a profound spiritual revival.

Following this, **Nehemiah**, a cupbearer to the Persian king, receives a divine burden to **rebuild Jerusalem's ruined walls.** His inspiring leadership, strategic prayer, and unwavering determination allow him to overcome intense opposition and complete the formidable task. Together, these books showcase God's faithfulness in fulfilling His promises to bring His people back, and they underscore the essential link between physical restoration and spiritual renewal, driven by dedicated leadership and a community committed to God's Word and purpose.

This week, we will explore the complementary stories of these two great leaders and the lessons embedded in their shared journey of rebuilding and renewal.

Devotional Thought: The Dual Work of Rebuilding – Brick by Brick, Heart by Heart

The books of Ezra and Nehemiah paint a vivid picture of restoration that is both practical and spiritual. Ezra prioritizes the rebuilding of the Temple and the spiritual foundation of God's Law, while Nehemiah tackles the seemingly impossible task of rebuilding the city walls, ensuring safety and identity. Neither's work was complete without the other. This dual effort reminds us that true, lasting restoration often requires attention to both the visible, tangible aspects of our lives and communities, and the invisible, spiritual foundations of faith and integrity.

The combined witness of Ezra and Nehemiah is profoundly encouraging. It calls us to engage in both the hard, visible work of building (brick by brick) and the vital, internal work of spiritual renewal (heart by heart), all while facing opposition with unwavering faith and strategic prayer.

This week, reflect on the areas in your life or community that need rebuilding. Are you attending to both the external structures and the internal spirit? How can you, like Ezra and Nehemiah, combine diligent effort with deep spiritual grounding to accomplish God's purposes for restoration?

Key Scriptures:

- **Ezra 1:1-4:** Cyrus's Decree and the First Return

- **Ezra 7:10:** Ezra's Dedication to Studying, Obeying, and Teaching the Law

- **Ezra 10:10-12:** The People's Repentance and Commitment to Renewal

- **Nehemiah 1:1-11:** Nehemiah's Prayer for Jerusalem

- **Nehemiah 2:17-20:** Nehemiah's Vision and Resolve to Rebuild the Walls

- **Nehemiah 4:6-9, 16-18:** Building with a Sword and a Trowel (Facing Opposition)

- **Nehemiah 8:1-8:** Ezra Reads the Law; The People Respond with Joy and Understanding

Reflection Questions:

1. The return from exile was a fulfillment of God's promises, despite the desolation they found. Where have you experienced God's faithfulness in bringing you through a season of "exile" or difficulty, into a place of hope and rebuilding?

2. Ezra's commitment to God's Law led to deep spiritual reform. How important is God's Word in your daily life as a guide for rebuilding and maintaining spiritual health, personally and communally?

3. Nehemiah's leadership involved both planning and intense prayer in the face of opposition. What challenging "walls" are you called to build in your life, and how can you emulate Nehemiah's blend of practical effort and spiritual reliance?

4. Both books highlight the importance of communal effort and overcoming internal and external obstacles. How can you contribute to building up your community, even when the task seems overwhelming or opposition arises?

5. Ezra and Nehemiah confronted various forms of sin and injustice among the people (e.g., intermarriage, economic exploitation). What responsibility do believers have to advocate for righteousness and justice within their spheres of influence today?

Week 12 Workbook

Date: _____

Key Takeaways from Devotional Thought:

_____

_____

_____

_____

_____

Insights from 1&2 Ezrah and Nehemiah:

_____

_____

_____

_____

_____

Devotional Reflection: How did this week's study deepen your understanding of spiritual reform?

_____

_____

_____

_____

_____

Week 13: Esther – Courage for a Time Such As This

The book of Esther stands unique among the historical books of the Old Testament. Set during the Persian exile, decades after the events of Ezra and Nehemiah, it tells the captivating story of a young Jewish woman named **Esther** who rises to become queen, and her cousin **Mordecai**. Remarkably, the name of God is never explicitly mentioned in the book. t His providential hand is evident throughout, orchestrating events to protect His people from annihilation. The plot revolves around a wicked official named Haman who devises a genocidal plan against the Jews.

Through Esther's courage, Mordecai's wisdom, and a series of "coincidences," Haman's plot is exposed and thwarted, leading to the deliverance of the Jewish people and the establishment of the festival of Purim. Esther is a powerful narrative of divine providence, human courage, and the responsibility to act faithfully in the face of injustice, even when the odds seem insurmountable.

This week, we will explore how God works behind the scenes, how one person's courage can change history, and the timeless call to rise up for "such a time as this."

Devotional Thought: Divine Providence and Courageous Action

"For if you remain silent at this time, relief and deliverance for the Jews will arise from another place, but you and your father's family will perish. And who knows but that you have come to your royal position for such a time as this?" (Esther 4:14). Mordecai's poignant challenge to Esther encapsulates the core message of this book. Despite the absence of God's name, His presence is undeniably felt as He orchestrates seemingly random events to protect His chosen people. Esther's decision to risk her life by approaching the king, after a period of prayer and fasting, is a powerful act of courage born from recognizing her divine purpose.

Esther's story resonates deeply. It reminds us that our positions, our gifts, and our very lives may be part of God's larger, providential plan to bring about deliverance and justice, often requiring us to step out in faith when it feels most daunting. This week, consider the "time such as this" in your own life or community. What injustice or challenge might God be calling you to address, and how can you step out in courageous faith, trusting in His unseen, powerful, hand?

Key Scriptures:

- **Esther 2:15-17:** Esther Becomes Queen
- **Esther 3:1-15:** Haman's Plot Against the Jews
- **Esther 4:1-3:** Mordecai's Mourning and Plea to Esther
- **Esther 4:13-16:** Mordecai's Challenge and Esther's Courageous Decision
- **Esther 5:1-3:** Esther Approaches the King
- **Esther 6:1-12:** The King Honors Mordecai
- **Esther 7:1-10:** Haman's Downfall
- **Esther 8:15-17:** Deliverance for the Jews

Reflection Questions:

1. Although God's name is not explicitly mentioned, His providence is evident throughout Esther. Where in your life have you seen God's unseen hand at work, orchestrating circumstances for good, even when His presence wasn't immediately obvious?

2. Esther faced a daunting decision: remain silent and safe, or risk her life to save her people. How do you discern when God is calling you to a courageous act, even when it involves personal risk?

3. Mordecai tells Esther she may have been placed in her position "for such a time as this." How can you recognize and utilize your unique gifts, position, or influence to serve God's purposes in your current circumstances?

4. The Jewish people responded to the threat with fasting and prayer before Esther's bold move. What role does spiritual preparation play in empowering you to face significant challenges?

5. Esther's story reminds us that seemingly small acts of obedience can have monumental consequences. How might your daily faithfulness contribute to God's larger plan of justice and redemption in the world around you?

Week 13 Workbook

Date: _____

Key Takeaways from Devotional Thought:

_____

_____

_____

_____

_____

Insights from Esther:

_____

_____

_____

_____

_____

Devotional Reflection: What Biblical insights on overcoming challenges did you gain from God's Word this week?

_____

_____

_____

_____

_____

_____

_____

_____

_____

Part 3: Wisdom and Poetry – The Heart's Cry and Life's Wisdom

After tracing the historical narrative of Israel from its origins to its return from exile, we now turn to a unique and deeply personal section of the Old Testament: **the Wisdom and Poetry books.** This collection, comprising Job, Psalms, Proverbs, Ecclesiastes, and Song of Solomon, shifts from chronicling events to exploring the profound questions of human experience, offering profound insights into life, suffering, faith, and love.

Through a rich tapestry of psalms, proverbs, philosophical reflections, and passionate poetry, these books give voice to the full spectrum of human emotion and grapple with timeless truths about God, humanity, and the meaning of existence. They invite us into intimate communion with God through worship, provide practical guidance for living wisely, and confront the mysteries of life's pain and pleasure.

This part will challenge us to feel deeply, think critically, and trust implicitly in the One who holds all wisdom.

Week 14: Job – Wrestling with Suffering and Sovereignty

The book of Job is a profound and often challenging exploration of human suffering, divine justice, and the nature of faith in the face of inexplicable pain. It introduces us to **Job,** a blameless and upright man who suddenly loses his wealth, his children, and his health, all while maintaining his integrity before God. The narrative quickly plunges into a series of dialogues between Job and his three friends (Eliphaz, Bildad, and Zophar) who arrive to comfort him but instead offer conventional, ultimately flawed, theological explanations for his suffering, largely insisting that Job must have sinned to deserve such calamity. Job vehemently defends his innocence and grapples with God's apparent silence and injustice, wrestling deeply with the concept of God's sovereignty.

The climax arrives when **God finally speaks** from a whirlwind, not to explain His actions, but to display His majestic power and wisdom, ultimately calling Job to trust in His unknowable ways. The book concludes with Job's humble repentance and restoration, not as a reward for his suffering, but as a demonstration of God's grace and redemptive power.

This week, we will journey with Job through his despair and doubt, seeking to understand the biblical perspective on suffering, the limits of human wisdom, and the ultimate comfort found in God's sovereign presence.

Devotional Thought: Finding Faith in the Whirlwind

Job's story is a raw and honest portrayal of what it means to suffer deeply, to question God, and, ultimately, to trust Him. His friends offered simplistic explanations, effectively telling him, "You must have done something wrong." But Job's unwavering conviction of his own innocence and his persistent cry to God highlight a crucial truth: **not all suffering is a direct result of personal sin.** Sometimes, suffering is a mystery, a test, or part of a larger divine purpose we cannot comprehend.

The book of Job offers a unique lens. It validates the cries of pain and the frustration with seemingly inexplicable hardships, while also pointing to a God who, even in His silence, is sovereign and worthy of trust. Job teaches us that it's okay to lament, to wrestle, and to question, but true faith holds onto God's character even when His actions are inscrutable. This week, reflect on the difficult questions or inexplicable pains you may carry. How can Job's journey encourage you to lament honestly, and still anchor your hope and trust in the vast, unsearchable wisdom and sovereignty of God, even when you're in the whirlwind?

Key Scriptures:

- **Job 1:1-22:** Job's Uprightness and Initial Losses
- **Job 2:7-10:** Job's Physical Affliction and His Wife's Counsel
- **Job 3:1-26:** Job's Lament and Curse of His Birth
- **Job 13:15:** Job's Declaration of Trust ("Though he slay me, yet will I hope in him")
- **Job 19:25-27:** Job's Hope in a Redeemer
- **Job 38:1-7:** God Answers Job from the Whirlwind (Beginning of God's speeches)
- **Job 40:1-5:** Job's Initial Response to God
- **Job 42:1-6:** Job's Repentance and Confession of God's Sovereignty
- **Job 42:10-17:** Job's Restoration and Blessing

Reflection Questions:

1. Job's friends offered various theological explanations for his suffering. How do these explanations often fall short when applied to real-life pain, and what does this teach us about our approach to comforting others?

---

2. Job never curses God, even in his deepest anguish. What does Job's perseverance in faith, despite intense suffering, teach you about maintaining integrity during trials?

3. God's response to Job (chapters 38-41) does not provide an explanation for his suffering but rather a majestic display of divine power and wisdom. How does this passage challenge your understanding of God's sovereignty and the limits of human comprehension?

4. Job declares, "Though he slay me, yet will I hope in him" (Job 13:15). In what areas of your life do you need to cultivate this level of trust in God?

5. Ultimately, Job is restored, but not as a direct "payment" for his endurance. What does this final restoration teach you about God's grace and His desire to redeem and bless, even beyond our understanding?

Week 14 Workbook

Date: _____

Key Takeaways from Devotional Thought:

_____

_____

_____

_____

_____

Insights from Job:

_____

_____

_____

_____

_____

Devotional Reflection: What Biblical insights on endurance did you gain from God's Word this week?

_____

_____

_____

_____

_____

_____

_____

_____

_____

Week 15: Psalms – The Spectrum of the Soul's Expression

The book of Psalms is the longest book in the Bible and stands as the heart of Old Testament worship. It is a collection of 150 poetic songs, prayers, and meditations that express the full range of human emotions and experiences, all directed towards God. Composed by various authors over centuries, with a significant portion attributed to King David, the Psalms cover themes of praise and worship, lament and sorrow, confession and repentance, thanksgiving, wisdom, historical reflection, and prophetic anticipation of the Messiah. They served as the hymnal and prayer book for ancient Israel, guiding their corporate and individual devotion.

The Psalms teach us how to approach God in every circumstance of life, offering a language for our deepest joys, our most profound pains, and our unwavering trust in His character.

This week, we will immerse ourselves in this rich tapestry of inspired poetry, learning how to express our souls honestly before God and finding comfort and strength in His enduring presence.

Devotional Thought: Every Emotion Welcome in His Presence

The Psalms are a profound invitation to bring our whole selves, our praise, our anger, our fear, our joy, our despair, to God. Psalmists cried out, "How long, Lord? Will you forget me forever?" (Psalm 13:1) and also declared, "The Lord is my shepherd; I shall not want" (Psalm 23:1). This radical honesty with God is a powerful model for us. For women who often carry immense burdens and are frequently expected to be "strong" even in the face of deep pain, the Psalms offer liberation.

They provide a sacred space where every emotion is not only acknowledged but validated as part of a real relationship with a sovereign God. The psalmists model for us how to lament without losing hope, how to praise in the midst of struggle, and how to find refuge in God even when the world feels chaotic.

This week, give yourself permission to be fully honest with God as you read the Psalms. What emotions are you holding back? How can the language of the Psalms help you articulate your deepest feelings to the One who hears and understands?

Key Scriptures:

- **Psalm 1:** The Way of the Righteous and the Wicked
- **Psalm 23:** The Lord is My Shepherd
- **Psalm 42:** Longing for God
- **Psalm 51:** A Prayer of Repentance
- **Psalm 90:** A Prayer of Moses, Man's Frailty and God's Eternity
- **Psalm 100:** A Psalm for Giving Thanks
- **Psalm 139:1-18:** God's Omnipresence and Omniscience
- **Psalm 145:** The Lord is Gracious and Compassionate
- **Psalm 150:** A Call to Praise the Lord

Reflection Questions:

1. The Psalms cover a wide range of emotions, from exuberant praise to deep lament. Which emotions do you find easiest to express to God, and which are most challenging? How can the Psalms help you grow in expressing your full emotional spectrum to Him?

2. Psalm 23 is a well-known passage of comfort and trust. What imagery or promises from this Psalm resonate most deeply with you in your current season of life?

3. Many Psalms are prayers of lament, expressing sorrow, anger, and confusion to God. What does this teach you about the acceptability of honest wrestling with God during times of suffering?

4. Psalm 139 speaks of God's intimate knowledge and presence. How does knowing that God fully sees and understands you, even your innermost thoughts, bring you comfort or challenge?

5. The Psalms repeatedly call us to praise God for His character and works. Beyond times of blessing, how can you cultivate a heart of praise even in challenging circumstances?

Week 15 Workbook

Date: _____

Key Takeaways from Devotional Thought:

_____

_____

_____

_____

_____

Insights from Psalms:

_____

_____

_____

_____

_____

Devotional Reflection: How did this week's study deepen your understanding of persistent prayer in difficult circumstances?

_____

_____

_____

_____

_____

_____

_____

_____

_____

Week 16: Proverbs – Wisdom for Everyday Living

The book of Proverbs is a collection of practical, God-given wisdom for navigating the complexities of daily life. Primarily attributed to **King Solomon**, renowned for his unparalleled wisdom, this book offers concise, memorable statements designed to instill discernment, knowledge, and understanding in those who seek it. Unlike the historical narratives or the emotional outpourings of the Psalms, Proverbs focuses on imparting skill in righteous living. It addresses a wide array of topics, from personal conduct, speech, and relationships to work ethic, financial management, and leadership.

The overarching theme is that **"the fear of the Lord is the beginning of wisdom"** (Proverbs 9:10). True wisdom, according to Proverbs, is not merely intellectual knowledge but a moral and spiritual understanding that leads to right choices and a life that honors God.

This week, we will delve into the timeless truths of Proverbs, discovering how ancient wisdom can powerfully guide our contemporary lives, helping us cultivate character, make sound decisions, and walk in integrity.

Devotional Thought: Practical Wisdom for a Purposeful Life

Proverbs cuts straight to the chase, offering clear guidance on how to live well in God's world. It's less about grand theological debates and more about the nitty-gritty of everyday choices: how to manage your tongue, handle money, treat your neighbor, and raise your children. It emphasizes that **wisdom is not just for the 'spiritual' moments, but for every single interaction and decision.**

For women, who often juggle multiple roles and responsibilities, from nurturing families to leading in their professions and communities, Proverbs provides an invaluable toolkit. It equips us to navigate complex relationships, speak with grace, work diligently, and build legacies of integrity. It reminds us that our daily faithfulness, even in seemingly small acts, contributes to a life of profound purpose and impact.

This week, consider a specific area of your life where you need practical wisdom. How can the teachings of Proverbs illuminate your path and empower you to make choices that reflect the fear of the Lord and lead to flourishing?

Key Scriptures:

- **Proverbs 1:7:** The Beginning of Knowledge
- **Proverbs 3:5-6:** Trust in the Lord with All Your Heart
- **Proverbs 4:23:** Guard Your Heart
- **Proverbs 10:19:** Wisdom in Words
- **Proverbs 15:1:** A Gentle Answer
- **Proverbs 16:3:** Commit Your Works to the Lord
- **Proverbs 22:6:** Train Up a Child
- **Proverbs 27:17:** Iron Sharpens Iron
- **Proverbs 31:10-31:** The Virtuous Woman (or Woman of Noble Character)

Reflection Questions:

1. Proverbs states that the fear of the Lord is the beginning of wisdom. What does "the fear of the Lord" mean to you in a practical sense, and how does it influence your pursuit of wisdom?
2. The book frequently contrasts the wise with the foolish. What characteristics define each, and how can you actively choose paths that lead to wisdom rather than folly?
3. Proverbs offers extensive counsel on the power of words. How can you apply these principles to your own communication, ensuring your speech is always gracious and life-giving?
4. Proverbs 3:5-6 encourages trusting in the Lord with all your heart, rather than relying on your own understanding. In what current

situations are you tempted to lean on your own understanding, and how can you intentionally surrender these to God?

5. The description of the virtuous woman in Proverbs 31 presents a multifaceted ideal of diligence, wisdom, and strength. Which aspects of her character particularly inspire you, and how can you cultivate them in your own life?

Week 16 Workbook

Date: _____

Key Takeaways from Devotional Thought:

_____

_____

_____

_____

_____

Insights from Proverbs:

_____

_____

_____

_____

Devotional Reflection: How did this week's study deepen your understanding of finding strength in God?

_____

_____

_____

_____

_____

_____

_____

_____

_____

Week 17: Ecclesiastes – The Meaning of Life Under the Sun

The book of Ecclesiastes is a profound and often perplexing exploration of life's meaning, purpose, and ultimate value. Attributed to "the Teacher" (traditionally identified as King Solomon in his old age), the book embarks on a relentless quest to find lasting satisfaction and significance "under the sun" that is, from a purely earthly perspective, without explicit reference to God's direct intervention or a clear afterlife. The Teacher meticulously examines every avenue humans typically pursue for fulfillment: wisdom, pleasure, wealth, hard work, success, and even righteousness.

His recurring conclusion is **"Vanity of vanities; all is vanity"** (Ecclesiastes 1:2), a declaration that everything ultimately proves to be futile, temporary, and unsatisfying. However, the book isn't nihilistic. It serves to dismantle our false idols and misplaced hopes, ultimately guiding us to a radical realization: true meaning and contentment are found only in **fearing God and keeping His commandments**, recognizing that our lives, and indeed all of creation, are ultimately in His hands.

This week, we will journey with the Teacher through his honest wrestling with life's enigmas, discovering that true wisdom lies not in grasping for fleeting pleasures, but in humble submission to our Creator.

Devotional Thought: Finding Purpose Beyond the Grind

"Meaningless! Meaningless! Utterly meaningless! Everything is meaningless." This stark declaration from Ecclesiastes can feel unsettling, but it perfectly captures the human struggle to find lasting purpose in a world filled with transient pursuits. The Teacher's journey to try everything "under the sun" to find fulfillment from accumulating knowledge to indulging in pleasure, ultimately leads to the conclusion that without a divine anchor, it all feels empty.

This book offers a crucial re-centering. It reminds us that even our most earnest efforts and achievements, if not rooted in God, can leave us feeling drained and unfulfilled. Ecclesiastes challenges us to look beyond the "grind" and the temporal rewards, and instead, find our ultimate satisfaction and purpose in a deeper relationship with our Creator.

This week, consider what you are striving for "under the sun." Are you finding true meaning, or a recurring sense of futility? How can the wisdom of Ecclesiastes prompt you to re-evaluate your priorities and anchor your pursuits in the fear of the Lord?

Key Scriptures:

- **Ecclesiastes 1:1-3, 9-11:** Introduction to the Teacher and the Cycle of Life
- **Ecclesiastes 2:1-11:** The Futility of Pleasure and Accomplishment
- **Ecclesiastes 3:1-8:** A Time for Everything
- **Ecclesiastes 5:10-12:** The Futility of Wealth
- **Ecclesiastes 7:1-4:** Wisdom in Sorrow
- **Ecclesiastes 9:11-12:** Time and Chance Happen to All
- **Ecclesiastes 11:9-12:1:** Advice to the Young; Remember Your Creator
- **Ecclesiastes 12:13-14:** The Conclusion of the Matter: Fear God and Keep His Commandments

Reflection Questions:

1. The Teacher experimented with various pursuits wisdom, pleasure, wealth to find meaning. Which of these pursuits do you often look to for fulfillment, and how has your experience mirrored the Teacher's conclusion of "vanity"?

2. Ecclesiastes 3:1-8 speaks of a time for everything. How does this perspective help you embrace the different seasons and paradoxes of life, trusting in God's timing?

3. The book suggests that true wisdom involves acknowledging life's uncertainties and injustices, rather than always seeking simple answers. How does this honest approach help you grapple with

difficult realities without losing faith?

4. The repeated phrase "under the sun" emphasizes a human, earthly perspective. What happens to our understanding of life's purpose when we lift our gaze beyond "under the sun" to God's eternal perspective?

5. The ultimate conclusion of Ecclesiastes is to fear God and keep His commandments. How does this final instruction provide true meaning and stability amidst the "vanity" of earthly life?

Week 17 Workbook

Date: _____

Key Takeaways from Devotional Thought:

_____

_____

_____

_____

_____

Insights from Ecclesiastes:

_____

_____

_____

_____

Devotional Reflection: How did this week's study deepen your understanding of what it means to live a life of faith?

_____

_____

_____

_____

_____

_____

_____

Week 18: Song of Solomon – The Allegory of Divine Love

The Song of Solomon, also known as the Song of Songs, stands as a uniquely poetic book within the biblical canon. While presented as a passionate dialogue between a man and a woman expressing deep romantic and sensual love, its profound significance, throughout centuries of Jewish and Christian tradition, lies in its allegorical interpretation.

In Judaism, the Song of Solomon is primarily understood as a rich symbol of the covenantal love and longing between God and the nation of Israel. Its expressions of yearning, separation, and intimate reunion beautifully mirror Israel's historical relationship with the Lord, especially through periods of exile and restoration.

In Christianity, this book is traditionally interpreted as depicting the fervent love between Christ and His Church, or between Christ and the individual believer's soul. The bride represents the Church (collectively) or the believer (personally), while the bridegroom is none other than Christ Himself.

Regardless of interpretation, the Song of Solomon unveils profound truths about the nature of deep, committed, and exclusive love. It celebrates mutual devotion, reverence, and faithfulness, inviting us to contemplate the unparalleled beauty of God's ardent love for His people and the Church's (or the believer's) devoted response. This week, we will immerse ourselves in this rich poetry, exploring its multifaceted expressions of love and its timeless lessons on the divine intimacy God desires with us.

Devotional Thought: Responding to the Lover of Our Souls

The Song of Solomon, when understood allegorically, is a profound testament to the passionate, pursuing love of God for His people. It reveals a divine Bridegroom (Christ) who delights in His bride (the Church/believer), longs for her presence, and offers intimate communion. This is not a distant, impersonal God, but one who expresses profound affection and desires deep relationship. In turn, the Song portrays the bride's longing, devotion, and faithfulness to her beloved.

This week, let this powerful allegory transform your understanding of God's love for you. How does the imagery of Christ as the ardent Bridegroom challenge or comfort you? Consider what it means to be cherished and pursued by the King of kings. How can your response reflect the bride's devotion – a love that is exclusive, unwavering, and deeply appreciative of His presence? The Song of Solomon encourages us to actively cultivate this intimate, exclusive devotion to the Lord, protecting our hearts for Him alone and delighting in His presence above all else.

Key Scriptures:

- Song of Solomon 1:2-4: The Bride's Longing for Her Beloved
- Song of Solomon 2:8-14: The Bridegroom's Call to Intimacy
- Song of Solomon 3:1-4: The Bride's Pursuit and Finding of Her Beloved
- Song of Solomon 4:7-12: The Bridegroom's Affirmation of the Bride's Beauty
- Song of Solomon 5:10-16: The Bride's Admiration for Her Beloved
- Song of Solomon 6:3: Mutual Possession ("I am my beloved's, and my beloved is mine")
- Song of Solomon 8:6-7: The Strength and Exclusivity of True Love
- Song of Solomon 8:13-14: The Concluding Longing for Communion

Reflection Questions:

1. Acknowledging the Song of Solomon's primary allegorical interpretation, what new insights did you gain about God's passionate love for His people (or Christ's love for the Church/believer)?

2. The Song portrays mutual longing and delight. How can you more intentionally express your devotion and longing for God's presence in your daily life?

3. Song of Solomon 8:6-7 describes love as strong as death and unquenchable. How does this verse, in an allegorical sense, speak to the enduring and unbreakable nature of God's covenant love for you?

4. The bride seeks her beloved and delights in His presence. How does this week's study encourage you to pursue a deeper, more intimate relationship with Christ, making Him your singular focus?

5. In what ways can the principles of exclusive devotion, faithfulness, and deep admiration, as portrayed in the Song of Solomon's allegory, be applied to your relationship with God?

Week 18 Workbook

Date: _____

Key Takeaways from Devotional Thought:

_____

_____

_____

_____

_____

Insights from Song of Solomon:

_____

_____

_____

_____

_____

Devotional Reflection: What Biblical insights did you gain from God's Word this week?

_____

_____

_____

_____

_____

_____

_____

_____

_____

_____

Part 4: The Major Prophets – Voices of Warning, Hope, and Future Glory

Following the deeply personal expressions of the Wisdom and Poetry books, we now transition to the powerful, often intense, words of **The Major Prophets**. This section introduces us to four pivotal figures, Isaiah, Jeremiah (along with Lamentations), Ezekiel, and Daniel, whose divinely inspired messages profoundly shaped the spiritual landscape of Israel and Judah. Spanning centuries of turmoil, from periods of national decline and impending judgment to the devastating Babylonian exile and the promise of return, these prophets served as God's spokespersons. They delivered stern warnings against idolatry

and injustice, called for sincere repentance, and, crucially, offered resounding messages of hope, restoration, and the ultimate coming of God's Messiah and His eternal kingdom.

This part will immerse us in the sweeping visions and challenging calls of these mighty prophets, revealing God's unwavering character, His justice, and His unfailing faithfulness to His covenant promises.

Week 19: Isaiah – The Prophet of Salvation and Kingly Glory

The book of Isaiah is often called the "fifth Gospel" due to its rich prophetic insights into the coming Messiah, even though it's set centuries before Jesus' birth. Spanning 66 chapters, it is one of the most comprehensive and magnificent books of prophecy in the Old Testament. **Isaiah** prophesied to the kingdom of Judah during a period of political instability and spiritual decline, urging them to trust in the Lord amidst alliances with foreign powers.

The book delivers a powerful dual message: it is a severe indictment of Judah's sin and idolatry, pronouncing divine judgment and the inevitability of exile; but equally, it overflows with glorious promises of God's future restoration, the coming of a righteous King (the Messiah), and the establishment of His universal kingdom. Isaiah speaks of a "Suffering Servant" who will bear the sins of many, and ultimately, of a new heavens and a new earth.

This week, we will delve into the profound depths of Isaiah's prophecy, discerning the patterns of God's judgment and grace, and marveling at the detailed foretelling of His ultimate plan of salvation.

Devotional Thought: Seeing God's Justice and Enduring Hope

Isaiah's prophecies are a whirlwind of divine majesty, stern warnings, and breathtaking promises. He confronts injustice head-on, condemning the exploitation of the poor and the hypocrisy of empty religious rituals. "Wash and make yourselves clean. Take your evil deeds out of my sight;

stop doing wrong. Learn to do right; seek justice. Defend the oppressed. Take up the cause of the fatherless; plead the case of the widow" (Isaiah 1:16-17).

Woven through these fiery pronouncements is an unwavering message of hope: God will ultimately bring justice, restore His people, and establish a kingdom where peace reigns.

Isaiah speaks directly to the soul. It validates the cries for justice while anchoring our hope in a God who is both righteous Judge and compassionate Redeemer. It reminds us that even in the darkest valleys, there is a promised future where God wipes away every tear.

This week, allow Isaiah's words to confront any complacency regarding injustice, while simultaneously strengthening your resolve to hope in God's ultimate justice and His glorious plan of salvation. How can you embody the call to seek justice and defend the oppressed, even as you rest in the certainty of God's sovereign plan?

Key Scriptures:

- **Isaiah 1:18:** Invitation to Repentance ("Come now, let us settle the matter")
- **Isaiah 6:1-8:** Isaiah's Vision and Call
- **Isaiah 7:14:** The Sign of Immanuel
- **Isaiah 9:6-7:** The Prophecy of the Messiah's Reign
- **Isaiah 26:3:** Perfect Peace for Those Whose Minds Are Steadfast
- **Isaiah 40:1-5:** Comfort for God's People; Prepare the Way of the Lord
- **Isaiah 40:28-31:** God's Strength for the Weary
- **Isaiah 53:1-12:** The Suffering Servant
- **Isaiah 55:1-3:** Invitation to Drink from the Water of Life
- **Isaiah 61:1-3:** The Anointed One's Mission (Prophecy of Jesus' Ministry)
- **Isaiah 65:17-25:** New Heavens and a New Earth

Reflection Questions:

1. Isaiah's prophecy combines strong pronouncements of judgment with glorious messages of hope. How does this tension reflect God's character and His dealings with humanity?

2. Isaiah 6 describes the prophet's encounter with God's holiness and his subsequent calling. What does this passage teach you about responding to God's call on your life, even when you feel inadequate?

3. The prophecies about the Messiah (like Isaiah 7:14, 9:6-7, 53) are central to understanding Jesus. Which of these prophecies particularly strengthens your faith in Jesus as the promised Savior?

4. Isaiah 40:28-31 promises renewed strength for those who wait on the Lord. In what areas of your life do you feel weary, and how can you practice "waiting on the Lord" to receive His strength?

5. Isaiah's consistent call for justice (e.g., Isaiah 1:16-17) is striking. How does this challenge you to advocate for justice and righteousness in your own sphere of influence and community?

Week 19 Workbook

Date: _____

Key Takeaways from Devotional Thought:

_____

_____

_____

_____

_____

Insights from Isaiah:

_____

_____

_____

_____

_____

Devotional Reflection: What Biblical insights on strengthening your faith did you gain from God's Word this week?

_____

_____

_____

_____

_____

Week 20: Jeremiah & Lamentations – The Prophet of Tears and Hope Amidst Despair

This week, we immerse ourselves in the poignant and powerful voice of **Jeremiah**, often known as the "weeping prophet," and the book of **Lamentations**, traditionally attributed to him. Jeremiah ministered during the tumultuous final decades of the kingdom of Judah, witnessing its spiritual decline, political instability, and eventual destruction by Babylon. His message was relentlessly challenging: a call to repentance, a stark warning of impending judgment, and a heartbreaking lament over Jerusalem's unfaithfulness. Despite constant persecution and rejection, Jeremiah faithfully delivered God's word, even as he himself endured profound personal suffering.

The book of Lamentations serves as a poetic dirge, a raw expression of grief and anguish over the destruction of Jerusalem and the suffering of its people during the exile. Even in its deepest despair, Lamentations clings to a glimmer of hope in God's unfailing love and compassion. Together, these books offer a profound meditation on the consequences of disobedience, the depth of divine judgment, and the persistent, redemptive hope found even in the midst of utter devastation.

Devotional Thought: Weeping with Hope, Enduring with Resilience

Jeremiah's life was a testament to enduring faithfulness in the face of immense pain and rejection. He loved his people deeply, even as he prophesied their downfall, and his tears over Jerusalem became emblematic of God's own sorrow. Lamentations echoes this grief, articulating the raw anguish of a people whose world has been shattered. "Because of the Lord's great love we are not consumed, for his compassions never fail. They are new every morning; great is your faithfulness" (Lamentations 3:22-23). This profound pivot from despair to hope, even in the ruins, is a beacon for us.

The narratives of Jeremiah and Lamentations offer permission to weep, to lament injustice, and to feel the weight of shattered dreams, without ever losing sight of God's enduring compassion. These books remind us that our resilience is rooted not in our own strength, but in God's faithfulness that is "new every morning." This week, consider the burdens you carry or the losses you grieve. How can the example of Jeremiah and the words of Lamentations empower you to express your lament honestly, while firmly anchoring your soul in the unfailing compassion and great faithfulness of God?

Key Scriptures:

- **Jeremiah 1:4-10:** Jeremiah's Call
- **Jeremiah 17:9-10:** The Deceitfulness of the Heart
- **Jeremiah 29:10-14:** Plans for Hope and a Future (Prophecy for the Exiles)
- **Jeremiah 31:31-34:** The New Covenant
- **Jeremiah 32:16-19, 26-27:** Jeremiah's Prayer and God's Response (Nothing is too hard for God)
- **Lamentations 1:1-7:** The Desolation of Jerusalem
- **Lamentations 3:19-24:** Hope in God's Unfailing Love
- **Lamentations 5:19-22:** A Plea for Restoration

Reflection Questions:

1. Jeremiah's message was largely one of impending judgment. He continued to preach it despite great personal cost. What does his faithfulness teach you about delivering difficult truths, even when they are unpopular?

2. Jeremiah 29:10-14 is a well-known passage of hope for the exiles. How do these verses speak to you about God's intentions for your future, especially when you feel displaced or in a difficult season?

3. The New Covenant promised in Jeremiah 31 fundamentally changes the relationship between God and His people. What

aspects of this covenant bring you the most hope and assurance today?

4. Lamentations paints a raw picture of suffering and grief. How does this book give you permission to lament honestly before God, even when your heart is broken?

5. Despite the profound suffering depicted, Lamentations pivots to hope in God's steadfast love and compassion (Lamentations 3:22-23). How can you cling to this truth when faced with despair or seemingly insurmountable challenges?

Week 20 Workbook

Date: _____

Key Takeaways from Devotional Thought:

_____

_____

_____

_____

_____

Insights from Jeremiah & Lamentations:

_____

_____

_____

_____

_____

Devotional Reflection: How did this week's study deepen your understanding of God's wisdom for navigating grief and disappointment?

_____

_____

_____

_____

_____

_____

_____

Week 21: Ezekiel – Visions of Glory, Judgment, and Restoration

The book of Ezekiel transports us into the turbulent world of the Babylonian exile, where the prophet **Ezekiel**, a priest, served as God's messenger to the Jewish captives. Unlike Jeremiah, who prophesied in Jerusalem before its fall, Ezekiel's ministry began among those already exiled. His book is characterized by vivid, often complex, symbolic visions, from the majestic cherubim and wheels (the "chariot throne" of God) to the valley of dry bones, each vision delivering a powerful message.

Ezekiel's prophecies address several critical themes: the **glory and holiness of God**, which had departed from the defiled Temple in Jerusalem; the **absolute certainty of divine judgment** on Judah and surrounding nations due to their idolatry and sin; and, ultimately, glorious promises of **future restoration**, including the re-establishment of the Temple, the spiritual renewal of the people (through the gift of a new heart and spirit), and the ultimate return of God's glory. Ezekiel's profound visions convey both the terrifying reality of God's wrath and the breathtaking scope of His redemptive plan.

This week, we will journey through Ezekiel's extraordinary revelations, grappling with the weight of God's judgment and celebrating the unfathomable hope of His restoration.

Devotional Thought: God's Presence Even in Exile

Ezekiel's ministry began in a foreign land, among a people stripped of their homeland, their Temple, and their perceived identity. They questioned if God was still with them, if He still cared, or if He even had power outside of Jerusalem. Ezekiel's visions emphatically answered these doubts: God's glory was not confined to Jerusalem; it moved with His people, even into exile (Ezekiel 10-11). This powerful truth, that God's presence and sovereignty transcend all circumstances, even the most desolate, is profoundly comforting.

Ezekiel offers a deep well of understanding. It acknowledges the pain of exile and loss, but firmly declares that God's presence remains, His glory travels with us, and His promises of renewal are steadfast, even when our circumstances feel like a "valley of dry bones." This week, reflect on areas in your life where you might feel "exiled," displaced, or disconnected. How can Ezekiel's visions remind you that God's glory is not bound by your location or circumstances, and that He is capable of bringing life and restoration even to the driest places?

Key Scriptures:

- **Ezekiel 1:4-28:** The Vision of God's Glory and Chariot Throne
- **Ezekiel 8:1-18:** The Abominations in the Temple
- **Ezekiel 11:17-20:** A New Heart and Spirit
- **Ezekiel 18:20-23, 30-32:** Individual Responsibility and God's Desire for Repentance
- **Ezekiel 33:10-11:** God's Desire for Repentance, Not Death
- **Ezekiel 36:24-28:** The Cleansing and Renewal of Israel
- **Ezekiel 37:1-14:** The Vision of the Valley of Dry Bones (Resurrection and Restoration)
- **Ezekiel 40-48:** The Vision of the New Temple (Future Worship and God's Presence)

Reflection Questions:

1. Ezekiel's visions of God's glory are awe-inspiring. How does understanding God's transcendent holiness and majesty impact your view of Him and your worship?
2. The book explicitly addresses individual responsibility (Ezekiel 18). How does this concept challenge the idea of collective guilt and emphasize personal accountability before God?
3. The "new heart and spirit" promised in Ezekiel 11 and 36 are foundational for the New Covenant. What does this spiritual transformation mean for your relationship with God today?

4. The vision of the valley of dry bones (Ezekiel 37) is a powerful metaphor for restoration. What "dry bones" or seemingly hopeless situations in your life or community do you need to speak God's word over, trusting in His power to bring life?

5. Ezekiel prophesied judgment. His ultimate message was one of restoration. How does this balance of divine justice and redemptive love shape your understanding of God's character and His plan for humanity?

Week 21 Workbook

Date: _____

Key Takeaways from Devotional Thought:

_____

_____

_____

_____

_____

Insights from Ezekiel:

_____

_____

_____

_____

Devotional Reflection: What biblical insights on spiritual renewal did you gain from God's Word this week?

_____

_____

_____

_____

_____

_____

_____

_____

Week 22: Daniel – Faithfulness in Exile and God's Sovereign Plan

The book of Daniel plunges us into the heart of the Babylonian exile, telling the remarkable story of **Daniel** and his three friends, Shadrach, Meshach, and Abednego, who demonstrate unwavering faithfulness to God amidst immense pressure in a foreign land. The book is divided into two main sections: the first six chapters narrate captivating stories of their courageous loyalty, such as Daniel in the lions' den, the fiery furnace, and the interpretation of Nebuchadnezzar's dreams. These narratives powerfully illustrate God's protection and sovereignty over human kingdoms.

The latter half of the book (chapters 7-12) contains highly symbolic and complex **prophetic visions** that reveal God's sovereign plan for the future, encompassing the rise and fall of empires, the ultimate triumph of God's eternal kingdom, and even detailed prophecies concerning the end times and the coming of the Messiah. Daniel offers profound lessons on living faithfully in a hostile culture, the ultimate authority of God, and the certainty of His unfolding purposes in history.

This week, we will explore Daniel's unwavering commitment and the breathtaking scope of God's sovereign control over nations and epochs.

Devotional Thought: Unwavering Faith in a Shifting World

Daniel and his friends faced an ultimate test of faith: compromise their convictions or face severe consequences, even death. Their courageous stand, refusing to defile themselves with the king's food or worship idols, speaks volumes about the power of unwavering commitment to God, no matter the cultural pressure.

Their stories, like the fiery furnace and the lions' den, are dramatic reminders that God is able to deliver those who trust Him, even miraculously. For women who often navigate spaces that demand conformity to oppressive norms or subtle compromises of faith, Daniel's example is incredibly potent. It highlights the importance of spiritual integrity, standing firm in conviction, and trusting that God sees, God hears, and God acts on behalf of His faithful. Daniel teaches us that our faithfulness in small, daily choices can prepare us for monumental stands, and that God's sovereign plan will unfold regardless of earthly powers.

This week, consider the "Babylon" in your own life: cultural pressures, workplace demands, or societal expectations that challenge your faith. How can Daniel's example inspire you to remain steadfast, trusting in God's power and His ultimate control over all circumstances?

Key Scriptures:

- **Daniel 1:8-20:** Daniel and His Friends' Resolve Not to Defile Themselves

- **Daniel 2:20-23:** Daniel Praises God for Wisdom and Revelation

- **Daniel 3:16-18:** Shadrach, Meshach, and Abednego Refuse to Worship the Idol

- **Daniel 3:24-28:** God Delivers Them from the Fiery Furnace

- **Daniel 4:34-35:** Nebuchadnezzar's Acknowledgment of God's Sovereignty

- **Daniel 6:10-23:** Daniel in the Lions' Den

- **Daniel 7:13-14:** The Vision of the Son of Man and His Everlasting Kingdom

- **Daniel 9:3-19:** Daniel's Prayer of Confession and Intercession

- **Daniel 12:2-3:** The Resurrection and Everlasting Life

Reflection Questions:

1. Daniel and his friends consistently chose faithfulness to God over cultural conformity or personal safety. In what areas of your life are you being challenged to stand firm in your convictions, and what courage can you draw from their example?

2. The narratives in Daniel consistently show God's power to deliver His faithful servants from impossible situations. How do these accounts strengthen your trust in God's ability to protect and intervene on your behalf?

3. Nebuchadnezzar's journey (Daniel 2, 4) highlights God's sovereignty over earthly kings and kingdoms. How does understanding God's ultimate control over global events bring you peace or challenge your perspective on current affairs?

4. Daniel's visions (chapters 7-12) reveal God's meticulous plan for the future. While some parts are complex, what overarching message of hope and God's ultimate victory do you take away from these prophecies?

5. Daniel's deep commitment to prayer is evident throughout the book. How does his consistent prayer life inspire you to deepen your own communion with God, especially during times of pressure or uncertainty?

Week 22 Workbook

Date: _____

Key Takeaways from Devotional Thought:

_____

_____

_____

_____

_____

Insights from Daniel:

_____

_____

_____

_____

_____

Devotional Reflection: What Biblical insights on hope for the future did you gain this week?

_____

_____

_____

_____

_____

_____

_____

_____

_____

_____

Week 23: Deeper Dive into a Major Prophetic Theme – The Day of the Lord

Having explored the individual voices of the Major Prophets, this week we'll take a "deeper dive" into a central and recurring theme that weaves through their prophecies: **The Day of the Lord**. This phrase, appearing frequently in Isaiah, Jeremiah, Ezekiel, and Daniel (and indeed, across the Minor Prophets and New Testament), is not just a single calendar day but a pivotal concept representing a time of **God's direct intervention in human history**. It signifies a period of both **judgment and salvation**, often characterized by dramatic cosmic and earthly disturbances, the downfall of wickedness, and the ultimate establishment of God's righteous rule. For some, it brings wrath and destruction; for others, it brings deliverance, restoration, and the dawn of a new era of peace and justice.

Understanding "The Day of the Lord" helps us grasp the prophets' urgent calls for repentance, their unwavering hope in God's ultimate triumph, and the future fulfillment of His promises. This week, we will synthesize insights from various prophetic books to build a comprehensive picture of this powerful theme, considering its past fulfillments, its future implications, and its relevance for our lives today.

Devotional Thought: Living in Light of God's Ultimate Justice

The concept of "The Day of the Lord" can initially sound daunting, evoking images of judgment and reckoning. However, for those who long for justice in a broken world, it is a message of profound hope. It assures us that God is not indifferent to suffering or injustice; He will ultimately set all things right. The prophets, in speaking of this day, not only warned against sin but also painted vivid pictures of restoration, peace, and the establishment of a perfect kingdom where "every knee shall bow."

"The Day of the Lord" offers powerful assurance that God's timeline is perfect, and His justice is certain. It strengthens our resolve to persevere in faith, knowing that the struggles we face "under the sun" are temporary, and God's ultimate victory is guaranteed. It calls us to live with intentionality, seeking righteousness and advocating for justice, as we await the full manifestation of His righteous reign.

This week, reflect on your understanding of God's justice. How does the prophetic theme of "The Day of the Lord" inspire you to live faithfully and hopefully, knowing that God will ultimately bring about perfect justice and restoration?

Key Scriptures (Synthesized from Major Prophets):

- **Isaiah 2:12-22:** The Lord Exalted on That Day (Judgment on the Proud)
- **Isaiah 13:6-13:** The Day of the Lord and the Fall of Babylon (Cosmic Disturbances)
- **Jeremiah 30:7-9:** Jacob's Trouble and Deliverance on That Day
- **Ezekiel 30:1-5:** The Day of the Lord on Egypt and Nations
- **Daniel 7:9-14:** The Ancient of Days and the Son of Man's Kingdom
- **Daniel 12:1-3:** Resurrection at the End of Days
- **Joel 2:1-2, 30-32 (Minor Prophet, but crucial for this theme):** The Day of the Lord is Great and Dreadful, but Deliverance for Those Who Call on Him.
- **Zephaniah 1:14-18 (Minor Prophet, also key):** The Great Day of the Lord, a Day of Wrath
- **Malachi 4:1-3 (Minor Prophet, also key):** The Day of the Lord Will Come, Burning Like a Furnace

Reflection Questions:

1. "The Day of the Lord" encompasses both judgment and salvation. How does this dual aspect of the theme reveal the complex nature of God's character (holy and just, merciful and redemptive)?

2. The prophets often described dramatic cosmic and earthly events associated with this day. How do these vivid descriptions impact your sense of God's power and ultimate authority over creation?

3. For whom is "The Day of the Lord" a message of dread, and for whom is it a message of hope? What does this distinction call you to consider about your own walk with God?

4. How does the certainty of "The Day of the Lord" motivate you to live a life of repentance, righteousness, and active faith today?

5. Reflect on the ultimate triumph of God's kingdom and the promise of a new heavens and a new earth found in the prophetic books. How does this ultimate hope shape your perspective on current struggles and future expectations?

Week 23 Workbook

Date: _____

Key Takeaways from Devotional Thought:

_____

_____

_____

_____

_____

Insights from this week's Bible study:

_____

_____

_____

_____

Devotional Reflection: How did this week's study deepen your understanding of the biblical concept of the "Day of the Lord"?

_____

_____

_____

_____

_____

_____

Part 5: The Minor Prophets – Concise Voices, Timeless Truths

As we move from the grand, sweeping narratives and extensive prophecies of the Major Prophets, we now enter the world of **The Minor Prophets**. Despite being labeled "minor" due to their shorter length, these twelve books are anything but insignificant. They deliver equally powerful and urgent messages from God, spanning centuries of Israel's and Judah's history, from periods of idolatry and social injustice to the aftermath of exile and the anticipation of the Messiah's coming.

These prophets acted as God's moral compass, challenging the people to return to covenant

faithfulness, condemning their sins, and simultaneously offering glimpses of divine judgment and glorious restoration. They speak to universal themes of God's unwavering love, His demand for justice, the consequences of sin, and the ultimate triumph of His righteous kingdom.

This section will demonstrate how God uses diverse voices, often in challenging circumstances, to speak profound truths that continue to resonate with clarity, confidence, and faith today.

Week 24: Prophetic Voices of Love & Justice (Hosea, Amos, Micah, Jonah)

This week, we will explore a selection of early Minor Prophets who powerfully championed two intertwined themes: **God's steadfast love (Hosea)** and His uncompromising demand for **justice (Amos, Micah)**, alongside the surprising story of **Jonah** that highlights God's universal compassion.

Hosea passionately portrays God's heartbroken love for His unfaithful people, using the metaphor of his own marriage to an unfaithful wife to illustrate Israel's spiritual adultery and God's persistent desire for reconciliation.

Amos, a shepherd from Judah, delivers fiery pronouncements against Israel's social injustice, economic exploitation, and religious hypocrisy, calling for righteousness to roll down like waters.

Micah echoes themes of judgment against injustice and idolatry, while also providing a famous prophecy of the Messiah's humble birthplace and a beautiful summary of what God truly requires.

Finally, the narrative of **Jonah** presents a prophet's reluctance to preach to Israel's enemies, underscoring God's expansive mercy even for those we deem unworthy. Together, these prophets reveal a God of both profound love and unwavering justice, demanding ethical living and compassionate hearts.

Devotional Thought: Love, Justice, and Compassion in Action

"He has shown you, O mortal, what is good. And what does the Lord require of you? To act justly and to love mercy and to walk humbly with your God" (Micah 6:8). This iconic verse encapsulates the heart of God's call found in these prophetic books. It's a call to move beyond empty rituals to a life deeply rooted in justice, compassion, and humble relationship with God. Hosea reminds us of the relentless, pursuing love of God even when we stray. Amos calls out the hypocrisy of those who claim to know God but oppress their neighbors. Jonah's story reveals God's boundless compassion, extending beyond our narrow prejudices.

For women who have often been at the forefront of movements for justice, equity, and compassionate care in their communities, these prophetic voices are deeply validating. They remind us that our fight for justice is God's fight, and our acts of love reflect His very character.

This week, reflect on how you embody justice, mercy, and humility in your daily life. Where is God calling you to stand up for righteousness, to extend compassion, or to walk more closely with Him in a world that desperately needs both His love and His justice?

Key Scriptures:

- **Hosea 3:1-5:** God's Redeeming Love for Unfaithful Israel
- **Hosea 6:6:** God Desires Steadfast Love, Not Sacrifice
- **Amos 5:21-24:** Let Justice Roll Down Like a River
- **Micah 5:2:** Prophecy of Bethlehem (Messiah's Birthplace)
- **Micah 6:8:** What the Lord Requires
- **Jonah 1:1-3:** Jonah's Disobedience
- **Jonah 3:1-10:** Nineveh's Repentance and God's Compassion
- **Jonah 4:9-11:** God's Concern for All Creation

Reflection Questions:

1. Hosea uses the metaphor of a broken marriage to illustrate Israel's relationship with God. How does this imagery help you understand God's persistent love for you, even when you are unfaithful?

2. Amos vehemently condemns social injustice. What forms of injustice do you see in your community or the world today, and how can you, like Amos, be a voice for righteousness?

3. Micah 6:8 is a powerful summary of God's requirements. Which of the three (acting justly, loving mercy, or walking humbly) do you find most challenging to practice consistently, and why?

4. Jonah's reluctance to preach to Nineveh highlights our own biases and God's expansive compassion. In what areas of your life might you be withholding compassion or judgment toward others whom God desires to reach?

5. Taken together, these prophets reveal a God who deeply cares about both our spiritual devotion and our ethical treatment of others. How can you better integrate love and justice into your personal faith and daily actions this week?

Week 24 Workbook

Date: _____

Key Takeaways from Devotional Thought:

_____

_____

_____

_____

Insights from this week's learning from minor prophets in the Bible:

_____

_____

_____

_____

Devotional Reflection: What did I learn this week about steadfast love?

_____

_____

_____

_____

_____

_____

Week 25: Prophetic Voices of Hope & Warning (Obadiah, Nahum, Habakkuk, Zephaniah)

This week, we continue our journey through the Minor Prophets, focusing on voices that delivered powerful messages of both impending **judgment and future hope**. These prophets ministered during a tumultuous period, as the Assyrian and Babylonian empires rose and threatened the nations around Judah, including Judah itself.

Obadiah, the shortest book in the Old Testament, delivers a stark prophecy against Edom for its pride and cruelty towards Judah during its distress, ensuring God's justice will prevail.

Nahum proclaims God's certain judgment against Nineveh, the mighty capital of Assyria, offering comfort to Judah that their oppressor will fall.

Habakkuk wrestles with profound questions of divine justice, questioning why God allows evil to prosper, and ultimately finds his resolution in trusting God's sovereignty even when understanding is elusive.

Finally, **Zephaniah** warns Judah of the coming "Day of the Lord," a day of wrath and destruction, but also includes promises of a remnant's restoration and the future joy of Jerusalem. Together, these prophets highlight God's righteous character, His control over nations, and His ultimate promise of salvation for those who remain faithful.

Devotional Thought: Finding Hope in God's Unwavering Justice

The prophets we study this week, while often delivering messages of warning and judgment, ultimately underscore a foundational truth: **God is just, and His purposes will prevail.** Obadiah and Nahum demonstrate that no nation, however mighty, can escape God's righteous judgment when they oppose His people or engage in evil. Habakkuk's honest wrestling with God's timing and methods ("How long, O Lord?") provides a powerful model for us when we struggle to understand suffering and injustice. His ultimate resolution to "rejoice in the Lord" even when circumstances are dire (Habakkuk 3:17-19) is a profound testament to faith.

These prophets offer a profound reassurance. They affirm that God hears every cry, and will ultimately bring about His perfect justice. They also call us to persevere in faith, to trust in God's sovereign plan, and to find joy in Him regardless of the outward circumstances. This week, what injustices weigh on your heart? How can the messages of these prophets bolster your hope in God's unwavering justice and empower you to trust His divine timing?

Key Scriptures:

- **Obadiah 1:15-21:** Edom's Judgment and Zion's Deliverance
- **Nahum 1:2-8:** God's Vengeance and His Goodness as a Stronghold
- **Nahum 3:1-7:** The Destruction of Nineveh
- **Habakkuk 1:2-4:** Habakkuk's Complaint to God
- **Habakkuk 2:2-4:** The Vision and the Just Shall Live by Faith
- **Habakkuk 3:17-19:** Rejoicing in the Lord Amidst Despair
- **Zephaniah 1:14-18:** The Great Day of the Lord's Wrath
- **Zephaniah 3:14-17:** Shout for Joy, O Daughter of Zion!

Reflection Questions:

1. Obadiah and Nahum focus on God's judgment against hostile nations. How does this demonstrate God's justice in holding all nations accountable, and what comfort does this bring concerning oppression today?

2. Habakkuk's dialogue with God is intensely honest about his confusion regarding injustice. When have you experienced similar questions or struggles with God's ways, and how might Habakkuk's

journey guide your own?

3. The phrase "the just shall live by his faith" from Habakkuk 2:4 is foundational. What does it mean to "live by faith" when circumstances seem bleak or contradictory to God's promises?

4. Zephaniah vividly describes the "Day of the Lord" as a day of wrath, but also of restoration. How does understanding both aspects of this divine intervention shape your perspective on repentance and hope?

5. Despite their challenging messages, these prophets ultimately point to God's unwavering control and His commitment to His people. How do these books strengthen your trust in God's sovereignty over all events, both good and bad?

Week 25 Workbook

Date: _____

Key Takeaways from Devotional Thought:

_____

_____

_____

_____

Insights from this week's learning about hope and warning in the Bible:

_____

_____

_____

_____

Devotional Reflection: How did this week's study deepen your understanding of salvation?

_____

_____

_____

_____

_____

_____

Week 26: Post-Exilic Promises (Haggai, Zechariah)

This week, we shift our focus to two Minor Prophets who ministered after the significant event of the Babylonian exile: **Haggai** and **Zechariah**.

These prophets played a crucial role in encouraging the returned exiles to rebuild the Temple in Jerusalem, a project that had stalled due to discouragement and opposition. Their messages are characterized by a strong emphasis on **reconstruction, spiritual renewal, and the future glory of God's restored people**. **Haggai** is remarkably direct and practical, rebuking the people for prioritizing their own homes over God's house and urging them to complete the Temple with renewed zeal, promising God's blessing. **Zechariah** offers a more extensive and symbolic set of visions, encouraging the builders with promises of divine assistance, the coming of the Messiah (depicted as both King and Priest), and the ultimate expansion of God's kingdom.

Together, Haggai and Zechariah serve as powerful reminders that God's promises of restoration are sure, and that His people are called to participate in His work with faithfulness and courage, even in the face of daunting challenges.

Devotional Thought: Rebuilding Faith in Seasons of Discouragement

Haggai and Zechariah spoke to a people who had returned home after decades of exile, only to find their land desolate and the task of rebuilding God's Temple overwhelming. They had grown discouraged, putting their own comforts before God's agenda. The prophets' message was clear: "Is it a time for you yourselves to be living in your paneled houses, while this house remains a ruin?" (Haggai 1:4). They reminded the people that God's presence and blessing were contingent upon their obedience and devotion. For women who often carry the burden of rebuilding, whether families, communities, or institutions, and can face immense discouragement and fatigue, the lessons from Haggai and Zechariah are invaluable.

They teach us that our efforts, though small, are significant when dedicated to God's purposes, and that God's Spirit is the ultimate source of strength for rebuilding: "Not by might nor by power, but by my Spirit,' says the Lord Almighty" (Zechariah 4:6).

This week, identify an area in your life, your family, or your community where you feel called to "rebuild" but might be discouraged. How can the promises in Haggai and Zechariah empower you to act with renewed faith, knowing that God's Spirit is at work and His ultimate plans for restoration will prevail?

Key Scriptures:

- **Haggai 1:1-11:** The Call to Rebuild the Temple
- **Haggai 2:6-9:** The Glory of the New Temple (Greater Than the Former)
- **Haggai 2:20-23:** God's Promise to Zerubbabel
- **Zechariah 1:1-6:** Call to Return to the Lord
- **Zechariah 4:6:** Not by Might, Nor by Power, but by My Spirit
- **Zechariah 8:3-8:** God's Promise to Restore Jerusalem
- **Zechariah 9:9-10:** The Coming King on a Donkey (Prophecy of Jesus' Triumphal Entry)
- **Zechariah 12:10:** Looking on the One They Have Pierced (Prophecy of Jesus' Crucifixion)
- **Zechariah 14:8-9:** The Lord Will Be King Over the Whole Earth

Reflection Questions:

1. Haggai directly challenges the people for their misplaced priorities. In what ways might you be prioritizing personal comfort or pursuits over God's will and work in your life today?
2. Zechariah 4:6 reminds us that true progress comes "not by might nor by power, but by my Spirit." How does this truth encourage you when facing tasks that seem too big for your own strength?

3. Both prophets offer visions of future glory for the Temple and Jerusalem. How do these prophecies of ultimate restoration provide hope and motivation for you in challenging times?

4. Zechariah contains several vivid prophecies about the Messiah, including His humble arrival and crucifixion. How do these specific details deepen your understanding of Jesus' identity and mission?

5. What small, faithful steps can you take this week to "rebuild" or contribute to God's purposes in an area where you've previously felt discouraged or stalled?

Week 26 Workbook

Date: _____

Key Takeaways from Devotional Thought:

_____

_____

_____

_____

Insights from this week's learning about Post-Exilic Promises:

_____

_____

_____

_____

Devotional Reflection: How did this week's study deepen your understanding of faithfulness and courage?

_____

_____

_____

_____

_____

_____

_____

_____

Week 27: Malachi – The Final Prophetic Voice and the Anticipation of Messiah

This week marks the conclusion of our journey through the Old Testament prophetic books with **Malachi**, the last voice in the Minor Prophets and the final book of the Old Testament before the 400-year period of silence leading up to the coming of John the Baptist and Jesus Christ. Malachi prophesied to a disheartened Jewish community that had returned from exile but had grown complacent and cynical in their worship and daily lives.

The book is structured as a series of disputations or dialogues between God and His people, where God raises accusations, the people question Him, and God responds with both rebuke and promise. Malachi confronts issues such as corrupt priesthood, faithless offerings, divorce, social injustice, and a general lack of reverence for God.

Amidst these strong rebukes, Malachi also delivers powerful promises: the coming of the "messenger" who will prepare the way for the Lord (prophetically pointing to John the Baptist), the "Sun of Righteousness" who will bring healing (the Messiah), and the ultimate **Day of the Lord** that will refine and restore God's faithful remnant. Malachi's urgent call for repentance and renewal serves as a bridge, looking back at Israel's covenant failures and looking forward to the fulfillment of God's redemptive plan in the New Testament.

Devotional Thought: Preparing Our Hearts for God's Arrival

Malachi speaks to a people who, despite having returned from exile, had fallen back into spiritual apathy. They were offering defiled sacrifices, treating their covenants lightly, and questioning God's justice. "Where is the God of justice?" they asked (Malachi 2:17), even as they practiced injustice themselves. Malachi's message is a wake-up call, emphasizing that true worship involves integrity in all areas of life, not just rituals. He also leaves us with the powerful anticipation of God's messenger and the "Sun of Righteousness" who will rise with healing in His wings.

Malachi calls us to examine our hearts, our worship, and our commitment to justice, ensuring our faith is vibrant and authentic. It also powerfully points us to the hope that is to come, the ultimate fulfillment of God's promises in Jesus. This week, consider areas in your spiritual life where complacency might have set in. How can Malachi's call for sincere worship and righteousness prepare your heart more fully for God's presence and His work in your life, as you anticipate the Day of the Lord?

Key Scriptures:

- **Malachi 1:6-10:** Rebuking Defiled Offerings
- **Malachi 2:13-16:** God's Hatred of Divorce and Treachery
- **Malachi 3:1-4:** The Messenger and the Lord's Coming to His Temple
- **Malachi 3:8-10:** Tithing and God's Blessing
- **Malachi 3:16-18:** The Book of Remembrance for Those Who Fear the Lord
- **Malachi 4:1-3:** The Day of the Lord Will Come, Burning Like a Furnace
- **Malachi 4:5-6:** Elijah's Return to Prepare the Way

Reflection Questions:

1. Malachi exposes the people's casual attitude toward God and their covenant obligations. In what ways might we, as modern believers, subtly dishonor God through our attitudes or actions?

2. Malachi 3:8-10 discusses tithing and offerings. How does this passage challenge your perspective on generosity and trusting God with your resources?

3. The concept of a "book of remembrance" for those who fear the Lord (Malachi 3:16) suggests God's attentive care for His faithful.

What comfort or challenge does this bring to your personal walk with God?

4. Malachi serves as the final Old Testament prophet, pointing forward to the coming of John the Baptist and Jesus. How does this bridge between the Old and New Testaments enhance your understanding of God's overarching plan of salvation?

5. What specific aspects of your spiritual life or daily conduct might God be calling you to refine or renew, inspired by Malachi's urgent call for repentance and reverence?

Week 27 Workbook

Date: _____

Key Takeaways from Devotional Thought:

_____

_____

_____

_____

Insights from Malachi:

_____

_____

_____

_____

Devotional Reflection: How did this week's study deepen your understanding of daily worship?

_____

_____

_____

_____

_____

_____

_____

_____

Part 6: The Gospels – The Life of Christ

As we conclude our journey through the Old Testament, we arrive at the most pivotal section of the biblical narrative: **The Gospels**. These four foundational books, Matthew, Mark, Luke, and John, are not merely historical biographies but divinely inspired accounts of the most significant life ever lived: that of Jesus Christ. They chronicle His miraculous birth, His powerful ministry of teaching and healing, His sacrificial death on the cross, and His glorious resurrection. The Gospels stand as the heart of the Christian faith, revealing God's ultimate act of love

and redemption through His Son.

Each Gospel writer, inspired by the Holy Spirit, offers a unique perspective and emphasis, painting a multifaceted portrait of Jesus as the promised Messiah, the Son of God, the Servant, and the Word made flesh.

This section marks a profound transition from the anticipation of redemption to its glorious realization, inviting us to encounter Jesus intimately and to understand the profound implications of His life for our own.

Week 28: Matthew – Jesus the King and the Kingdom of Heaven

The Gospel of **Matthew** serves as a vital bridge between the Old and New Testaments, presenting Jesus primarily as the long-awaited **Messiah and King**, the fulfillment of God's promises to Israel. Written likely for a Jewish Christian audience, Matthew meticulously connects Jesus' life and ministry to Old Testament prophecies, beginning with His genealogy tracing back through David and Abraham. Key features of this Gospel include: the profound teachings of the **Sermon on the Mount** (chapters 5-7), extensive parables illustrating the nature of the **Kingdom of Heaven**, and a strong emphasis on Jesus' authority as a teacher and miracle-worker. Matthew frequently highlights Jesus' role as the new Moses, bringing a new and higher law, and culminates with the Great Commission, sending His disciples to make disciples of all nations.

This week, we will explore Matthew's deliberate presentation of Jesus as the promised King, the one who inaugurates God's reign and calls His followers to live as citizens of His eternal Kingdom.

Devotional Thought: The Kingdom of Heaven: God's Present Reign

Matthew's Gospel repeatedly proclaims the "Kingdom of Heaven," a central theme defining Jesus' ministry. This is the present reality of God's sovereign rule breaking into human hearts and history, impacting every aspect of life. Jesus, the King, embodies liberation from sin's power, delivering profound teachings that welcome all who repent, elevate those whom society overlooks, and perfectly define true righteousness according to God's character.

His Sermon on the Mount (Matthew 5-7) isn't abstract philosophy; it's a blueprint for living out transformed lives within the Kingdom, demonstrating the spiritual character of those who truly belong to God's reign. Here, the poor in spirit, the meek, and those who hunger for righteousness are blessed, reflecting a righteousness that flows from a heart submitted to God.

Matthew's portrayal of Jesus as the righteous King who inaugurates this Kingdom is incredibly empowering. It reminds us that God's reign is not distant but active in the lives of believers, and we are called to live in a way that reflects its transformative power on earth. This week, what does it mean for you to live as a citizen of the Kingdom of Heaven today? How can Jesus' teachings and His example as King inspire you to pursue personal righteousness, embrace repentance, and live out God's will in your sphere of influence?

Key Scriptures:

- **Matthew 1:1-17:** Jesus' Genealogy, Tracing to Abraham and David
- **Matthew 1:18-25:** The Birth of Jesus (Immanuel)
- **Matthew 2:1-12:** The Visit of the Magi
- **Matthew 3:13-17:** Jesus' Baptism
- **Matthew 4:1-11:** Jesus' Temptation in the Wilderness
- **Matthew 5:1-12:** The Beatitudes (Sermon on the Mount)
- **Matthew 6:9-13:** The Lord's Prayer (Sermon on the Mount)
- **Matthew 7:24-29:** The Wise and Foolish Builders (Sermon on the Mount Conclusion)
- **Matthew 13:44-46:** Parables of the Kingdom (Hidden Treasure and Pearl)
- **Matthew 16:13-20:** Peter's Confession of Christ
- **Matthew 25:31-46:** The Parable of the Sheep and the Goats (Judgment)
- **Matthew 27:32-54:** The Crucifixion of Jesus
- **Matthew 28:16-20:** The Great Commission

Reflection Questions:

1. Matthew emphasizes Jesus' fulfillment of Old Testament prophecies. How does this consistent theme strengthen your faith in the Bible's divine inspiration and God's sovereign plan?

2. The Sermon on the Mount (Matthew 5-7) presents radical ethical teachings. Which of these teachings challenges you most to live differently as a citizen of the Kingdom of Heaven?

3. Jesus' parables often reveal the nature of the Kingdom. Which parable in Matthew has particularly impacted your understanding of God's reign or your role within it?

4. Matthew's Gospel frequently highlights Jesus' authority. How does His authority as King and Teacher bring you comfort, guidance, or conviction in your daily life?

5. The Great Commission (Matthew 28:18-20) calls us to make disciples. How can you actively participate in fulfilling this commission in your unique context, sharing the message of Jesus the King?

Week 28 Workbook

Date: _____

Key Takeaways from Devotional Thought:

_____

_____

_____

_____

_____

Insights from Matthew:

_____

_____

_____

_____

_____

Devotional Reflection: What Biblical insights on impacting the world around you did you gain this week?

_____

_____

_____

_____

_____

_____

_____

_____

_____

Week 29: Mark – Jesus the Suffering Servant and Son of God

Continuing our exploration of the Gospels, this week we turn to the Gospel of **Mark**, widely considered the earliest and shortest of the four Gospel accounts. Mark presents Jesus as the **Suffering Servant** and the **powerful Son of God**, emphasizing His actions and immediate impact rather than lengthy discourses. Characterized by its fast-paced narrative, often using the word "immediately," Mark dives directly into Jesus' public ministry after His baptism, showcasing His divine authority through numerous miracles, exorcisms, and confrontations with religious leaders.

Mark also highlights the disciples' struggles to understand Jesus' true identity and mission, particularly His path to suffering and sacrifice. The Gospel builds towards the dramatic climax of Jesus' crucifixion and His triumphant resurrection, solidifying His identity as the Christ, the Son of God, even in suffering.

This week, we will discover Mark's dynamic portrayal of Jesus' active ministry, His call to radical discipleship, and the profound significance of His ultimate sacrifice.

Devotional Thought: Following the Path of the Servant

Mark's Gospel confronts us with a Jesus who is constantly in motion, serving, healing, and confronting evil. Paradoxically, Mark also emphasizes Jesus' journey towards suffering and sacrifice, the **Suffering Servant** who came "not to be served but to serve, and to give his life as a ransom for many" (Mark 10:45). This model of leadership and life calls for radical discipleship, where following Jesus means embracing self-denial and carrying our own crosses (Mark 8:34). For those who are called to lead, serve, and make a difference in challenging environments, Mark's Gospel provides a powerful example. It reminds us that true authority often comes through humble service, and that our greatest impact may emerge not from seeking power or recognition, but from sacrificial love and unwavering commitment to God's will, even when it leads through difficult paths.

This week, reflect on areas in your life where God is calling you to serve. How does Jesus' example as the Suffering Servant in Mark challenge your understanding of power, purpose, and discipleship?

Key Scriptures:

- **Mark 1:1-15:** John the Baptist Prepares the Way; Jesus' Baptism and Temptation
- **Mark 1:21-28:** Jesus Teaches with Authority and Casts Out an Impure Spirit
- **Mark 2:1-12:** Jesus Heals a Paralytic and Forgives Sins
- **Mark 4:35-41:** Jesus Calms the Storm
- **Mark 5:25-34:** The Woman with the Issue of Blood
- **Mark 8:27-30:** Peter's Confession of Christ
- **Mark 8:34-38:** Taking Up Your Cross
- **Mark 10:42-45:** Servant Leadership
- **Mark 14:32-42:** Jesus in Gethsemane
- **Mark 15:33-39:** The Crucifixion and the Centurion's Confession
- **Mark 16:1-8:** The Resurrection

Reflection Questions:

1. Mark's Gospel is known for its fast pace. How does this emphasis on action and immediacy draw you into Jesus' ministry?

2. Jesus performs many miracles in Mark. Which miracle particularly stands out to you, and what does it reveal about Jesus' power and compassion?

3. The disciples in Mark often struggle to understand Jesus' mission and identity. How do their struggles resonate with your own journey of faith and understanding?

4. Mark frequently highlights Jesus' path to suffering. What does Jesus' willingness to suffer teach you about true strength and obedience to God's will?

5. What specific actions or attitudes of Jesus in Mark's Gospel inspire you to live a more committed and sacrificial life of discipleship?

Week 29 Workbook

Date: _____

Key Takeaways from Devotional Thought:

_____

_____

_____

_____

_____

Insights from Mark:

_____

_____

_____

_____

_____

Devotional Reflection: How did this week's study deepen your understanding of the triumph of the resurrection?

_____

_____

_____

_____

_____

_____

_____

_____

_____

Week 30: Luke – Jesus the Compassionate Savior of All

Moving into the third Synoptic Gospel, this week we explore the Gospel of **Luke**. Written by Luke, a Gentile physician and companion of Paul, this Gospel is unique for its extensive research, meticulous detail, and a deliberate focus on presenting Jesus as the **compassionate Savior for all humanity**, particularly for the marginalized, the poor, women, and outcasts.

Luke's Gospel begins with the most detailed account of Jesus' birth and early life, and it's also the longest of the Gospels, providing a rich narrative that emphasizes Jesus' humanity, His prayer life, and the role of the Holy Spirit in His ministry. Key themes include: God's salvation extending beyond Israel to the Gentiles, the radical inclusion of the outcast, the importance of prayer, the joy of the Gospel, and the emphasis on social justice. Luke's portrayal of Jesus highlights His empathy, His interactions with Samaritans, tax collectors, and sinners, and His unwavering love for those often overlooked by society.

This week, we will immerse ourselves in Luke's beautiful narrative, appreciating the breadth of God's redemptive plan and Jesus' profound compassion for every person.

Devotional Thought: God's Heart for the Marginalized

Luke's Gospel offers a profound and beautiful picture of Jesus' heart for those on the fringes of society. Time and again, Jesus is found interacting with, healing, and elevating the status of the poor, the sick, the demon-possessed, and those considered societal outcasts tax collectors, Samaritans, and women.

He tells parables like the Good Samaritan and the Prodigal Son, illustrating radical compassion and forgiveness. This emphasis on **inclusion and compassion** is a powerful affirmation that God's love and salvation are for *everyone*, regardless of social standing, ethnicity, or past mistakes. For anyone who has ever felt overlooked, marginalized, or excluded, Luke's Gospel speaks directly to your experience. It reminds us that God sees the unseen, values the devalued, and passionately pursues the lost. It calls us to embody that same compassion, actively seeking out and showing love to those who are often forgotten or mistreated in our own communities.

Where can you apply the principles of God's inclusive love and compassion this week? How does Jesus' example in Luke inspire you to reflect God's mercy and extend care to those often overlooked, demonstrating the transforming power of the Gospel? This week, where can you practice radical inclusion? How does Jesus' example in Luke inspire you to extend compassion and advocate for those who are marginalized in the world around you?

Key Scriptures:

- **Luke 1:26-38:** The Annunciation to Mary
- **Luke 2:1-20:** The Birth of Jesus and the Shepherds' Visit
- **Luke 4:16-30:** Jesus' Sermon in Nazareth and His Mission Statement (quoting Isaiah 61)
- **Luke 7:36-50:** The Anointing of Jesus by a Sinful Woman
- **Luke 10:25-37:** The Parable of the Good Samaritan
- **Luke 15:11-32:** The Parable of the Prodigal Son
- **Luke 18:9-14:** The Parable of the Pharisee and the Tax Collector
- **Luke 19:1-10:** Zacchaeus the Tax Collector
- **Luke 23:32-43:** Jesus Forgives the Thief on the Cross
- **Luke 24:13-35:** The Road to Emmaus
- **Luke 24:44-53:** The Great Commission and Ascension

Reflection Questions:

1. Luke provides the most detailed account of Jesus' birth and early life. What new insights or appreciation do you gain from these narratives about Jesus' humanity and divine purpose?

2. Jesus frequently interacts with the poor, the sick, and societal outcasts in Luke. How do these interactions challenge your understanding of who God seeks to save and use?

3. Prayer is a recurring theme in Luke's Gospel, with Jesus often seen praying before significant events. How does Jesus' example inspire your own prayer life, especially during important moments?

4. Luke includes parables unique to his Gospel, such as the Good Samaritan and the Prodigal Son. What enduring lessons about compassion, forgiveness, and God's love do you draw from these stories?

5. How does Christ's sovereign mission, as revealed in Luke 4:18-19, compel you to participate in extending God's grace and light in your sphere of influence?

Week 30 Workbook

Date: _____

Key Takeaways from Devotional Thought:

_____

_____

_____

_____

_____

Insights from Luke:

_____

_____

_____

_____

_____

Devotional Reflection: What Biblical insights on compassion did you gain from God's Word this week?

_____

_____

_____

_____

_____

_____

_____

_____

_____

_____

Week 31: John – Jesus the Son of God, the Word Incarnate

Concluding our study of the four Gospels, this week we turn to the Gospel of John, a unique and profound account that stands apart from the three Synoptic Gospels (Matthew, Mark, and Luke). John's Gospel does not focus on historical chronology or parables as much as it emphasizes the divine identity of Jesus as the eternal Son of God, the "Word made flesh." From its opening declaration in John 1:1, "In the beginning was the Word, and the Word was with God, and the Word was God," John immediately proclaims Jesus' co-existence and co-equality with God the Father.

This Gospel presents key declarations where Jesus describes His nature and purpose, such as, "I am the Bread of Life," "I am the Light of the World," and "I am the Way, the Truth, and the Life." These are profound statements revealing Jesus' divine attributes and His essential role in God's plan. John also records fewer but longer discourses of Jesus, focusing on deep theological truths, and highlights significant miracles (often called "signs") designed to elicit faith in Jesus as the Christ, the Son of God, so that through believing, people may have eternal life. This week, we will delve into John's rich theological narrative, encountering Jesus not just as a historical figure, but as the very embodiment of God, the source of eternal life and truth.

Devotional Thought: Understanding Christ's Divine Nature

John's Gospel invites us to a deep understanding of Jesus' divine nature, revealing Him not merely as a great teacher or a compassionate Savior, but as the divine Son of God, eternally existing with the Father. The statements where Jesus declares His identity and provision are particularly powerful. He proclaims Himself as the source of spiritual sustenance ("the Bread of Life"), the guide through darkness ("the Light of the World"), the ultimate Shepherd, the resurrection and the life, the sole path to the Father, the embodiment of truth, and the true vine from whom all life flows.

This profound theological understanding of Jesus' divinity is not abstract; it deeply impacts how we live and believe. If Jesus is God incarnate, then His words carry ultimate authority, and His sacrifice possesses infinite power to atone for sin. For all seeking to deepen their understanding of God and the vastness of His love, John's Gospel offers an unparalleled journey into the heart of Jesus' divine identity. It calls us to move beyond mere intellectual assent to a living, abiding faith that transforms our very being.

Key Scriptures:

- **John 1:1-18:** The Word Became Flesh
- **John 2:1-11:** Jesus Changes Water into Wine (First Sign)
- **John 3:16-17:** God So Loved the World
- **John 4:7-26:** Jesus and the Samaritan Woman
- **John 6:35:** "I Am the Bread of Life"
- **John 8:12:** "I Am the Light of the World"
- **John 10:9-11:** "I Am the Gate" and "I Am the Good Shepherd"
- **John 11:25-26:** "I Am the Resurrection and the Life"
- **John 13:1-17:** Jesus Washes the Disciples' Feet
- **John 14:6:** "I Am the Way, the Truth, and the Life"
- **John 15:1-5:** "I Am the True Vine"
- **John 17:1-26:** Jesus' High Priestly Prayer
- **John 19:28-30:** "It is Finished" (Crucifixion)
- **John 20:24-29:** Thomas Believes
- **John 20:30-31:** The Purpose of John's Gospel

Reflection Questions:

1. John's Gospel begins by declaring Jesus as "the Word" who "was with God, and was God" (John 1:1). What does this foundational truth reveal about Jesus' eternal nature and His relationship with God the Father?

2. Jesus makes several profound declarations about His identity and purpose (e.g., "I am the Bread of Life," "I am the Light of the World," "I am the Way, the Truth, and the Life"). Choose one of these declarations and explain what it reveals about who Jesus is and what He provides.

Week 31 Workbook

Date: _____

Key Takeaways from Devotional Thought:

_____

_____

_____

_____

Insights from John:

_____

_____

_____

_____

Devotional Reflection: How did this week's study deepen your understanding of eternal life as revealed in Scripture?

_____

_____

_____

_____

_____

_____

_____

_____

_____

Part 7: The Early Church

Our journey through the New Testament now shifts from the pivotal life, ministry, death, and resurrection of Jesus Christ to the incredible story of what happened *after* He ascended to heaven.

Part 7: The Early Church delves into the foundational book of Acts, which chronicles the birth, growth, and initial spread of Christianity. This section is vital for understanding how the message of Jesus, empowered by the Holy Spirit, moved from a small group of disciples in Jerusalem to reach the farthest corners of the Roman Empire. We

will witness the miraculous outpouring of the Holy Spirit, the bold proclamation of the Gospel by the apostles, the formation of diverse communities of believers, and the challenges (both internal and external) faced by the nascent church.

Through Acts, we see the Church's divine origin, its Spirit-driven mission, and the unwavering commitment of its early leaders to fulfill Christ's Great Commission, laying the groundwork for all future generations of believers.

Week 32: Acts – The Birth and Spread of the Early Church (Acts 1-28)

This week, we embark on the fascinating and foundational book of **Acts**, a vital historical account that bridges the Gospels with the Pauline and General Epistles. Acts, often referred to as the "Acts of the Apostles" or, more accurately, the "Acts of the Holy Spirit," narrates the momentous period following Jesus' ascension to heaven.

We will cover the **entire book of Acts this week as an overview**, understanding its narrative flow, central themes, and key figures. The book begins with the promise of the Holy Spirit and the momentous outpouring at Pentecost, leading to the birth of the Church. It then traces the rapid, Spirit-empowered expansion of the Gospel message from Jerusalem, through Judea and Samaria, and ultimately to the capital of the Roman Empire, Rome itself.

We will observe how ordinary individuals, empowered by the Holy Spirit, faced opposition, performed miracles, established new communities of believers, and navigated groundbreaking decisions like the inclusion of Gentiles into the Christian fold. Acts reveals the power of God at work in and through His people, demonstrating the unstoppable nature of His redemptive plan.

Devotional Thought: The Spirit-Driven Mission

The Book of Acts is a testament to the **power and direction of the Holy Spirit in initiating and propelling God's mission.** From the disciples' waiting for the promise of the Spirit (Acts 1), to the dramatic Pentecost event (Acts 2), and through every subsequent bold sermon, miraculous healing, and challenging journey, the Holy Spirit is the true protagonist of Acts. He transforms timid followers into courageous witnesses, breaks down cultural and social barriers, and ensures the Gospel is proclaimed to all nations.

Acts reminds us that the Church's strength lies not in human programs or charisma, but in its absolute reliance on the indwelling and empowering presence of the Holy Spirit. It challenges us to surrender our plans to His leading, to trust in His guidance, and to step out in faith, knowing that the same Spirit who enabled the early church to turn the world upside down is alive and active in us today.

This week, consider how the Holy Spirit moved through the early church. In what ways are you depending on the Holy Spirit for guidance and empowerment in your own life and in your contribution to God's mission?

Key Scriptures:

- **Acts 1:1-11:** Jesus' Farewell and the Promise of the Holy Spirit
- **Acts 2:1-47:** Pentecost and the Birth of the Church
- **Acts 3:1-4:31:** Healing and Early Persecution of Peter and John
- **Acts 6:1-7:60:** The Appointment of Deacons and Stephen's Martyrdom
- **Acts 8:1-40:** Persecution Scatters Believers; Philip's Ministry
- **Acts 9:1-31:** The Conversion of Saul (Paul)
- **Acts 10:1-48:** Peter and Cornelius: The Gospel for Gentiles
- **Acts 13:1-3:** Paul's First Missionary Journey Begins
- **Acts 15:1-35:** The Jerusalem Council and Gentile Inclusion
- **Acts 16:6-40:** The Macedonian Call and Ministry in Philippi
- **Acts 17:1-34:** Paul's Ministry in Thessalonica, Berea, and Athens
- **Acts 18:1-21:** Paul in Corinth
- **Acts 19:1-41:** Paul in Ephesus

- **Acts 20:17-38:** Paul's Farewell to the Ephesian Elders
- **Acts 21:1-23:35:** Paul's Return to Jerusalem and Arrest
- **Acts 24:1-26:32:** Paul's Trials Before Felix, Festus, and Agrippa
- **Acts 27:1-28:31:** Paul's Voyage to Rome and Ministry There

Reflection Questions:

1. How does the Book of Acts demonstrate the fulfillment of Jesus' promise to send the Holy Spirit, and what was the immediate impact of the Spirit's arrival at Pentecost?

2. The early church grew exponentially despite intense persecution. What factors, empowered by the Holy Spirit, do you believe were most crucial for their remarkable growth?

3. Acts details the expansion of the Gospel from a Jewish context to include Gentiles. What challenges and breakthroughs did the early church experience in bridging these cultural and religious divides?

4. Consider the courage and boldness of figures like Peter, Stephen, and Paul in sharing their faith, even in the face of threats. How can their examples inspire your own evangelism today?

5. What overarching lesson about God's sovereignty and the Church's mission do you take away from reading the entire Book of Acts this week?

Week 32 Workbook

Date: _____

Key Takeaways from Devotional Thought:

_____

_____

_____

_____

Insights from Acts:

_____

_____

_____

_____

Devotional Reflection: What Biblical insights on redemption did you gain from God's Word this week?

_____

_____

_____

_____

_____

_____

_____

_____

_____

_____

Part 8: The Pauline Epistles

Having explored the birth and initial spread of the early church in Acts, we now turn our attention to the pivotal collection of letters penned by one of Christianity's most influential figures: the **Apostle Paul. Part 8: The Pauline Epistles** will systematically delve into thirteen (or fourteen, including Hebrews, depending on theological perspective) powerful and foundational letters that shaped early Christian theology and practice, and continue to guide believers today.

Written to various churches and individuals across the Roman

Empire, these epistles address critical doctrines like **justification by faith, the nature of the Holy Spirit, the unity of the church as the body of Christ, and the hope of Christ's return.** Beyond theology, Paul's letters offer immensely practical guidance on Christian living, addressing issues of ethics, relationships, worship, and discipleship within the burgeoning Christian communities.

As we journey through these inspired writings, we'll gain a profound understanding of the Gospel's implications for both belief and behavior, directly from the pen of the apostle uniquely called to bring the message of Christ to the Gentile world.

Week 33: Romans – The Gospel of God's Righteousness

This week, we begin our deep dive into the Pauline Epistles with the magnificent **Book of Romans**, widely considered Paul's most comprehensive and systematic theological treatise. Written to the church in Rome, a congregation Paul had not yet visited, this letter lays out the foundational truths of the Christian faith in unparalleled depth. We will explore Paul's profound explanation of the **Gospel of God's righteousness**, beginning with the universal reality of sin and humanity's need for salvation. Paul meticulously argues that **justification (being declared righteous before God) comes not through adherence to the Law, but solely by grace through faith in Jesus Christ.**

We will delve into key themes such as the power of the Gospel, the reconciliation of humanity to God through Christ's death and resurrection, the role of the Law, the significance of Abraham's faith, the believer's new life in the Spirit, God's faithfulness to Israel, and practical exhortations for Christian living. Romans serves as a powerful reminder of God's perfect justice and His boundless love revealed in the saving work of Christ.

Devotional Thought: The Power of the Gospel

Paul begins Romans by declaring his eagerness to preach the Gospel, stating it is "the power of God for salvation to everyone who believes" (Romans 1:16). This is the **dynamic, transformative power of God** that radically changes human lives.

The core of this Gospel, as Romans powerfully articulates, is that while humanity is utterly lost in sin and incapable of earning God's favor, God, in His infinite love, has provided a way for us to be declared righteous through faith in Jesus Christ. This truth liberates us from the burden of trying to earn our salvation and empowers us to live a new life by the Spirit. Romans invites us to marvel at the depth of God's grace and to fully grasp the liberating truth that our righteousness comes not from our own efforts, but from Christ alone.

This week, as you study Romans, consider the profound truth that the Gospel is God's power for *your* salvation. How does the doctrine of justification by faith alone impact your daily walk with God? In what ways does understanding God's righteousness deepen your gratitude and fuel your desire to live a life that honors Him?

Key Scriptures:

- **Romans 1:16-17:** The Power of the Gospel
- **Romans 3:9-26:** All Are Under Sin; Righteousness Through Faith
- **Romans 5:1-11:** Peace and Reconciliation Through Christ
- **Romans 6:1-14:** Dead to Sin, Alive in Christ
- **Romans 7:1-8:17:** The Struggle with Sin and Life in the Spirit
- **Romans 8:18-39:** Future Glory and God's Unfailing Love
- **Romans 9:1-11:36:** God's Righteousness and Israel's Place in His Plan
- **Romans 12:1-21:** Living a Transformed Life; Christian Conduct
- **Romans 13:1-7:** Submission to Governing Authorities
- **Romans 14:1-15:13:** Living Together in Unity and Love
- **Romans 15:14-16:27:** Paul's Ministry Plans and Greetings

Reflection Questions:

1. Paul argues that "all have sinned and fall short of the glory of God" (Romans 3:23). How does understanding the universality of sin highlight the necessity and beauty of God's grace?

2. The concept of "justification by faith" is central to Romans. What does it mean to you to be declared righteous by God, not based on your works, but on faith in Christ's work?

3. How does Romans describe the transformation that occurs when a believer is united with Christ in His death and resurrection (Romans 6)? What practical implications does this have for your daily life?

4. Romans 8 speaks powerfully about "no condemnation" and "life in the Spirit." What comfort and assurance do you find in these verses regarding your standing before God and the Spirit's work in you?

5. Romans 12:1-2 calls believers to "offer your bodies as a living sacrifice." How does Paul connect profound theological truth to practical, ethical living in the concluding chapters of Romans?

Week 33 Workbook

Date: _____

Key Takeaways from Devotional Thought:

_____

_____

_____

_____

_____

Insights from Romans:

_____

_____

_____

_____

_____

Devotional Reflection: How did this week's study deepen your understanding of God's righteousness?

_____

_____

_____

_____

_____

_____

_____

_____

Week 34: 1 & 2 Corinthians – Practical Christianity in a Fractured Church

This week, we move from the theological profundity of Romans to the intensely practical and pastoral challenges faced by the church in Corinth, as addressed in **1 and 2 Corinthians**. These two letters reveal a vibrant but deeply flawed Christian community situated in a major, cosmopolitan, and morally corrupt Roman city.

1 Corinthians tackles a wide array of practical issues: divisions and factions within the church, sexual immorality, lawsuits among believers, questions about marriage, food offered to idols, the proper conduct of worship (including spiritual gifts and the Lord's Supper), and the crucial doctrine of the resurrection. Paul's guidance is firm and loving, aimed at restoring unity, purity, and proper order in the church.

2 Corinthians is a more personal and emotionally charged letter, where Paul defends his apostleship against false teachers, expresses his deep affection for the Corinthian believers, and emphasizes the nature of true Christian ministry, marked by suffering, humility, and the power of God. Together, these letters provide invaluable insights into the complexities of church life and the enduring principles for living out the Gospel in a challenging cultural context.

Devotional Thought: God's Grace for Imperfect People

The Corinthian church was a messy, human community, filled with squabbles, moral failings, and misunderstandings. It was a church that Paul deeply loved and tirelessly discipled. The Corinthian letters offer immense encouragement because they demonstrate that **God's grace extends not only to save us but also to sanctify us in our ongoing brokenness**. Paul doesn't abandon the Corinthians; he patiently, sometimes sternly, but always lovingly, calls them back to Christ and to godly living. He reminds them of their identity "in Christ" and challenges them to live up to that high calling.

For us, 1 and 2 Corinthians reveal that church is a hospital for sinners, not a museum for saints. It reminds us that unity is precious, purity is essential, and genuine spiritual power comes through humility and faithfulness.

This week, as you read about the Corinthian church's struggles and Paul's guidance, consider your own church community. Where can you extend grace? How can you contribute to unity and health? And how does Paul's example encourage you in confronting challenges with love and truth, trusting in God's power to perfect His people?

Key Scriptures (Focus on representative passages from both letters):

- **1 Corinthians 1:10-17:** Divisions in the Church
- **1 Corinthians 5:1-13:** Dealing with Immorality
- **1 Corinthians 6:12-20:** Sexual Immorality and the Body as a Temple
- **1 Corinthians 10:23-11:1:** Freedom and Responsibility (Food offered to idols)
- **1 Corinthians 12:1-31:** Spiritual Gifts and the Unity of the Body of Christ
- **1 Corinthians 13:1-13:** The Supremacy of Love
- **1 Corinthians 15:1-58:** The Resurrection of Christ and Our Resurrection
- **2 Corinthians 1:3-11:** God of All Comfort in Suffering
- **2 Corinthians 3:1-18:** The New Covenant and the Spirit's Ministry
- **2 Corinthians 5:11-21:** The Ministry of Reconciliation

- **2 Corinthians 8:1-15:** Principles of Generosity
- **2 Corinthians 10:1-11:15:** Paul Defends His Apostleship
- **2 Corinthians 12:1-10:** Paul's Thorn in the Flesh and God's Grace

Reflection Questions:

1. What were some of the main problems Paul addressed in the Corinthian church, and what do these reveal about the challenges early Christian communities faced?

2. In 1 Corinthians 12-14, Paul discusses spiritual gifts. What is the overarching principle he emphasizes regarding their use in the church? How can this be applied today?

3. 1 Corinthians 13, the "love chapter," is famous. How does Paul define biblical love, and how does this definition challenge or affirm your understanding of love within the Christian community?

4. 2 Corinthians is deeply personal, with Paul defending his ministry. What does this letter teach us about the marks of genuine spiritual leadership and the nature of suffering for Christ?

5. Both letters offer strong practical guidance. Choose one specific piece of advice from either 1 or 2 Corinthians that you find particularly relevant to your own life or church community right now.

Week 34 Workbook

Date: _____

Key Takeaways from Devotional Thought:

_____

_____

_____

_____

Insights from Corinthians:

_____

_____

_____

_____

Devotional Reflection: How did this week's study deepen your understanding of God's love?

_____

_____

_____

_____

_____

_____

_____

_____

_____

Week 35: Galatians & Ephesians – Freedom in Christ & Unity in the Body

This week, we delve into two powerful and foundational Pauline Epistles: **Galatians and Ephesians.** Though distinct in their primary focus, both letters profoundly articulate the nature of salvation by grace through faith and its implications for the Christian life.

Galatians is often called Paul's "Magna Carta of Christian Liberty." Written in response to Judaizers who were teaching that Gentile converts must observe aspects of the Jewish Law (like circumcision) to be truly saved, Paul vehemently defends the doctrine of **justification by faith alone, apart from works of the Law.** This letter is a passionate declaration of the freedom believers have in Christ from the bondage of legalism and a powerful reminder that salvation is a gift received through faith, not earned by human effort.

Ephesians, in contrast, is a majestic and highly theological letter that focuses on the **riches of God's grace in Christ and the unity of the Church.** Paul emphasizes God's eternal plan of salvation, the incredible spiritual blessings believers have in Christ, and the profound mystery of Jew and Gentile being united into one new humanity the Church the body of Christ. The second half of the letter moves from theological truth to practical application, urging believers to "walk worthy" of their calling, living in unity, purity, and spiritual warfare. Together, these letters provide a balanced and comprehensive view of God's grace, our freedom in

Christ, and our identity and purpose as part of His glorious Church.

Devotional Thought: Living in Liberty and Unity

Galatians is a powerful reminder that the Gospel of grace sets us truly free. It frees us from the impossible burden of earning God's favor through our own efforts and from the legalistic tendencies that can creep into faith. Our salvation is a pure gift, received through simple faith in Christ's finished work. This liberty, however, is not a license for sin but an empowerment to live by the Spirit, producing genuine righteousness and love. Ephesians then beautifully paints the picture of what this freedom *leads to*: profound unity within the Church. God's ultimate purpose is to bring all things together in Christ, reconciling diverse peoples into one body, built on love and grace.

For us today, these letters challenge us to firmly reject any form of legalism that diminishes the sufficiency of Christ's work and to actively pursue unity and purity within the body of Christ.

This week, reflect on the freedom you have in Christ. How does understanding justification by faith alone impact your joy and security? How can you contribute to the unity and health of your church, living out your identity as a cherished member of Christ's body?

Key Scriptures:

- **Galatians 1:6-9:** No Other Gospel
- **Galatians 2:15-21:** Justification by Faith, Not by Works of the Law
- **Galatians 3:1-14:** Law or Faith? Abraham's Example
- **Galatians 5:1-6:** Freedom in Christ
- **Galatians 5:16-26:** Living by the Spirit (Fruit of the Spirit)
- **Galatians 6:1-10:** Bear One Another's Burdens
- **Ephesians 1:3-14:** Spiritual Blessings in Christ
- **Ephesians 2:1-10:** By Grace Through Faith
- **Ephesians 2:11-22:** One New Humanity in Christ
- **Ephesians 3:1-13:** The Mystery Revealed to Paul
- **Ephesians 4:1-16:** Unity in the Body of Christ
- **Ephesians 4:17-5:21:** Living a New Life in Christ
- **Ephesians 6:10-20:** The Armor of God

Reflection Questions:

1. How does Paul's strong warning against a "different gospel" in Galatians 1 relate to the importance of guarding the purity of the Gospel message today?

2. What does Galatians teach us about the relationship between "faith" and "works" in our salvation and sanctification?

3. Ephesians describes incredible "spiritual blessings" that believers have in Christ (Ephesians 1:3-14). Which of these blessings resonates most deeply with you, and why?

4. How does Ephesians powerfully illustrate the unity that Christ brings between different groups of people (e.g., Jew and Gentile, male and female, slave and free) within the Church? What practical steps can you take to promote this unity in your context?

5. Ephesians 6 introduces the "Armor of God." What is the significance of each piece of the armor, and how can you actively "put on" this armor in your daily life?

Week 35 Workbook

Date: _____

Key Takeaways from Devotional Thought:

_____

_____

_____

_____

_____

Insights from Galatians & Ephesians:

_____

_____

_____

_____

_____

Devotional Reflection: What Biblical insights on resilience did you gain this week?

_____

_____

_____

_____

_____

_____

_____

_____

_____

_____

Week 36: Philippians & Colossians – Joy in Christ & Supremacy of Christ

This week, our exploration of the Pauline Epistles brings us to two more profound letters written by Paul during his imprisonment: **Philippians and Colossians**. Though both are "prison epistles," they offer distinct, complementary insights into the Christian life.

Philippians is often called the "Epistle of Joy." Despite being in chains, Paul writes with infectious joy and deep affection to the church in Philippi, his first church plant in Europe. This letter overflows with themes of **Christ-like humility, the pursuit of joy in all circumstances, the importance of unity in the Gospel, and the confident expectation of Christ's return.** Paul urges believers to live out their salvation with practical righteousness, emphasizing the humility of Christ as the ultimate example for their conduct.

Colossians is a powerful theological letter that champions the **supremacy and sufficiency of Christ.** Paul wrote to counter false teachings in Colossae that were diminishing Christ's unique role and promoting human philosophies, legalism, and mystical experiences. He boldly proclaims Christ as the creator, sustainer, and head of all things, in whom "all the fullness of God dwells." This letter underscores that believers are complete in Christ, needing nothing more, and calls them to live out this new identity by setting their minds on things above and putting off the old self. Together, these letters provide a compelling vision of the Christian life centered on the person and work of Jesus Christ, offering joy and completeness found nowhere else.

Devotional Thought: Finding Completeness and Joy in Christ Alone

Paul's ability to exude **joy** from a Roman prison (Philippians) is a powerful testimony to the source of his strength: his deep relationship with Jesus Christ. His joy was not circumstantial but Christ-centered, found in the partnership of the Gospel and the assurance of God's sovereign plan. This profound joy is intertwined with the message of **Colossians**, which declares that **Christ is supremely sufficient for all our needs.**

In Him, we "have been given fullness" (Colossians 2:10). We don't need human philosophies, rituals, or mystical experiences to complete us; Christ alone is everything. For us today, these letters offer a liberating truth: true joy is found in knowing and following Christ regardless of our circumstances, and true completeness comes from Him alone, freeing us from the endless pursuit of external validation or self-improvement apart from Him.

This week, consider what fills you with joy. Are you pursuing external things or finding your deepest joy in Christ? How does knowing that you are "complete in Christ" impact your view of yourself and your pursuits?

Key Scriptures:

- **Philippians 1:1-11:** Paul's Affection and Prayer for the Philippians
- **Philippians 1:12-30:** Christ Proclaimed in All Circumstances
- **Philippians 2:1-11:** Christ's Humility: The Mind of Christ
- **Philippians 2:12-18:** Working Out Your Salvation
- **Philippians 3:1-11:** Righteousness Through Faith in Christ
- **Philippians 4:4-7:** Rejoice in the Lord Always; Peace of God
- **Philippians 4:10-20:** Contentment in Every Circumstance
- **Colossians 1:15-23:** The Supremacy of Christ
- **Colossians 2:6-15:** Complete in Christ; Freedom from Legalism
- **Colossians 3:1-17:** Set Your Minds on Things Above; Put on the New Self
- **Colossians 3:18-4:6:** Household Codes and Christian Conduct
- **Colossians 4:2-6:** Persistence in Prayer and Wise Conduct

Reflection Questions:

1. How does Paul's example in Philippians demonstrate that joy is possible even in difficult circumstances? What is the source of his joy?

2. Philippians 2:5-11 presents the profound "Christ Hymn" on humility. How does Christ's example of humility challenge your own attitudes and actions?

3. Colossians strongly emphasizes the "supremacy" of Christ. What specific aspects of Christ's person and work are highlighted in this letter?

4. Paul warns against "empty deceit" and human philosophies in Colossians. How might believers today be susceptible to similar diversions that diminish Christ's sufficiency?

5. Both letters move from profound theology to practical application. Choose one practical exhortation from either Philippians or Colossians that you want to intentionally apply to your life this week.

Week 36 Workbook

Date: _____

Key Takeaways from Devotional Thought:

_____

_____

_____

_____

_____

Insights from Philippians:

_____

_____

_____

_____

_____

Devotional Reflection: What Biblical insights on joy did you gain this week?

_____

_____

_____

_____

_____

_____

_____

_____

_____

Week 37: 1 & 2 Thessalonians – Enduring Hope and Godly Living

This week, we turn our attention to **1 and 2 Thessalonians**, two of Paul's earliest letters, written to a relatively young church in Thessalonica. These letters offer a unique glimpse into the practical concerns and vibrant faith of new believers, as well as Paul's profound pastoral heart.

1 Thessalonians is a letter of commendation, encouragement, and instruction. Paul praises the Thessalonians for their enduring faith, love, and hope despite persecution, reminding them of his affection and the purity of his ministry among them. The letter also provides crucial teaching on living a life that pleases God, with an emphasis on sexual purity, brotherly love, hard work, and, most notably, the **second coming of Christ.** Paul reassures believers about those who have died in Christ and clarifies the events surrounding the Lord's return.

2 Thessalonians builds upon the first letter, addressing persistent misunderstandings and new concerns within the community. Paul clarifies further details about the **Day of the Lord**, correcting false teaching that the day had already come. He also confronts idleness and encourages diligent work, reminding believers to persevere in well-doing despite growing persecution. Together, these letters provide vital comfort regarding Christ's return, practical guidance for daily Christian living, and a strong call to steadfastness in faith.

Devotional Thought: Living with Eternal Perspective

The Thessalonian letters stand out for their strong emphasis on eschatology, the study of end times and Christ's return. Paul constantly points the Thessalonians to the coming of the Lord, using this truth as a powerful motivator for holy living, patient endurance, and evangelism. He reassures them about the destiny of those who have died in Christ and corrects misunderstandings that caused anxiety. For us today, 1 and 2 Thessalonians offer a crucial reminder to live with an **eternal perspective**. Our hope is not in this fleeting world, but in the glorious return of our Saviour.

This hope should inspire us to live lives of purity, diligence, and brotherly love, knowing that our labour in the Lord is not in vain. This week, as you read these letters, how does the promise of Christ's return shape your priorities and daily decisions? How can focusing on eternal hope help you endure current difficulties and live more faithfully for God?

Key Scriptures:

- **1 Thessalonians 1:2-10:** Commendation for Faith, Love, and Hope

- **1 Thessalonians 2:1-12:** Paul's Ministry Among Them

- **1 Thessalonians 4:1-12:** Call to Holy Living, Purity, and Love

- **1 Thessalonians 4:13-18:** The Lord's Coming and the Resurrection of the Dead

- **1 Thessalonians 5:1-11:** The Day of the Lord and Living Soberly

- **1 Thessalonians 5:12-28:** Final Exhortations and Benediction

- **2 Thessalonians 1:3-12:** Praise for Perseverance; God's Just Judgment

- **2 Thessalonians 2:1-17:** The Man of Lawlessness and the Day of the Lord

- **2 Thessalonians 3:1-5:** Prayer Requests and God's Faithfulness

- **2 Thessalonians 3:6-15:** Warning Against Idleness

- **2 Thessalonians 3:16-18:** Final Prayer and Blessing

Reflection Questions:

1. How did the Thessalonians' faith and love serve as an example to other believers (1 Thess 1:7-8)? What qualities of their church stand out to you?

2. Paul addresses sexual purity and brotherly love in 1 Thessalonians 4. Why are these aspects of Christian living so important, especially for new believers?

3. Both letters discuss the return of Christ. What comforting truths about Christ's return do you find in these passages, particularly regarding those who have died?

4. Paul corrects misunderstandings about the Day of the Lord in 2 Thessalonians 2. What practical dangers arise when people are misinformed about end-time events?

5. What instructions does Paul give regarding those who are idle or refuse to work (2 Thess 3:6-12)? How can these principles be applied in our communities today?

Week 37 Workbook

Date: _____

Key Takeaways from Devotional Thought:

_____

_____

_____

_____

_____

Insights from Thessalonians:

_____

_____

_____

_____

_____

Devotional Reflection: How did this week's study deepen your understanding of perseverance?

_____

_____

_____

_____

_____

_____

_____

_____

_____

Week 38: 1 & 2 Timothy & Titus – Leadership and Godliness in the Church

This week, we turn to Paul's final letters, often referred to as the **Pastoral Epistles: 1 Timothy, 2 Timothy, and Titus.** These deeply personal and practical letters were written to Paul's closest companions and spiritual sons, providing crucial guidance for effective leadership and sound doctrine within the burgeoning early churches.

1 Timothy is Paul's guide for Timothy, who was leading the church in Ephesus. It addresses issues of false teaching, the conduct of public worship, the qualifications for elders and deacons, and instructions for various groups within the church. Paul emphasizes the importance of a leader's character and the foundational truths that combat doctrinal error, ensuring a healthy and well-ordered church.

2 Timothy is Paul's final letter, written from a Roman prison, anticipating his imminent martyrdom. It's a poignant and powerful call for Timothy to **persevere in the Gospel,** to guard the truth, to faithfully teach and preach the Word, and to endure suffering for Christ. Paul passes on the torch of ministry, urging Timothy to remain faithful and to raise up others who will do the same.

Titus was written to Paul's associate on the island of Crete, where Titus was tasked with organizing and establishing churches. This letter provides practical instructions for appointing qualified leaders, dealing with rebellious people, and teaching sound doctrine that leads to **godly living**. It connects theological truth directly to observable character and behavior, emphasizing that the grace of God has appeared, bringing salvation and training us to live disciplined and godly lives. Together, these three epistles offer an indispensable manual for church leadership, theological integrity, and the pursuit of practical godliness in every believer's life.

Devotional Thought: Faithfulness in Leadership and Life

The Pastoral Epistles underscore a critical truth: **sound doctrine is inseparable from godly living, and faithful leadership is essential for a healthy church**. Paul doesn't just tell Timothy and Titus what to believe; he tells them how to live, how to lead, and how to train others to do the same. He emphasizes character, integrity, and perseverance, knowing that leaders set the tone for the entire flock. In 2 Timothy, Paul's final charge to Timothy to "preach the Word" and to "endure hardship" serves as a powerful call to faithfulness for all believers, not just leaders.

These letters challenge us to examine our own lives: are we living consistently with the truth we claim to believe? Are we, in whatever sphere of influence we have, faithfully stewarding the Gospel and living lives that commend Christ to others?

This week, reflect on the qualities of godly leadership and living described in these letters. How can you, in your own sphere, demonstrate faithfulness to the Gospel and a commitment to practical godliness?

Key Scriptures:

- **1 Timothy 1:3-7:** Warning Against False Teaching
- **1 Timothy 2:1-8:** Instructions for Public Worship and Prayer
- **1 Timothy 3:1-13:** Qualifications for Overseers and Deacons
- **1 Timothy 4:6-16:** A Good Minister of Christ Jesus; Train for Godliness
- **1 Timothy 6:6-19:** Godliness with Contentment; The Love of Money
- **2 Timothy 1:6-14:** Guard the Good Deposit; Fan into Flame Your Gift
- **2 Timothy 2:1-13:** Entrust to Faithful Men; Endure Hardship
- **2 Timothy 2:14-26:** Handle the Word Accurately; A Workman Approved

- **2 Timothy 3:10-17:** All Scripture is God-Breathed
- **2 Timothy 4:1-8:** Paul's Charge to Timothy; His Imminent Departure
- **Titus 1:5-9:** Qualifications for Elders
- **Titus 2:1-10:** Sound Doctrine for Godly Living in Various Groups
- **Titus 2:11-15:** The Grace of God Brings Salvation and Trains Us
- **Titus 3:3-8:** Saved by God's Mercy, Not by Works

Reflection Questions:

1. Why does Paul place such a strong emphasis on the character and qualifications of church leaders in these letters? How do these qualifications apply to leaders today?

2. What false teachings did Paul warn against in 1 Timothy and Titus, and how do these contrast with sound doctrine? What are some contemporary parallels?

3. In 2 Timothy, Paul encourages Timothy to "fan into flame the gift of God" and "guard the good deposit." What do these phrases mean, and how can you apply them to your own spiritual gifts and understanding of truth?

4. How do these letters connect theological truth (e.g., the grace of God, Christ's death) directly to practical, godly living in the community? Provide specific examples.

5. Paul's final charge to Timothy in 2 Timothy 4:1-5 is a powerful call to faithful ministry. What aspects of this charge resonate most with you, and how might you respond to it in your own life?

Week 38 Workbook

Date: _____

Key Takeaways from Devotional Thought:

_____

_____

_____

_____

_____

Insights from Timothy & Titus:

_____

_____

_____

_____

_____

Devotional Reflection: How did this week's study deepen your understanding of how to remain steadfast in faith?

_____

_____

_____

_____

_____

_____

_____

_____

_____

_____

Week 39: Philemon & Practical Application of Grace

This week, we conclude our direct study of Paul's individual letters by focusing on a remarkable short epistle: **Philemon**. Often overlooked due to its brevity, this letter provides a profound and intensely personal illustration of the **practical application of grace, reconciliation, and the transformative power of the Gospel** in real-life relationships.

The letter to **Philemon** is a plea from Paul to a wealthy Christian slave owner named Philemon, on behalf of his runaway slave, Onesimus, who had encountered Paul and become a believer in Christ. Paul appeals to Philemon not with apostolic authority or command, but with tender persuasion, asking him to receive Onesimus back not merely as a slave, but as a "beloved brother" in Christ.

This letter beautifully exemplifies Christian love, forgiveness, and the way the Gospel breaks down social barriers, elevating even the lowest members of society to equal standing within the family of God. It's a powerful narrative of how theological truth translates into radical, grace-filled action in our daily interactions.

Devotional Thought: Grace That Transforms Relationships

The letter to Philemon is a powerful micro-example of the grand truths of the Gospel we've seen throughout Paul's epistles. It's a demonstration of **grace in action**: Paul doesn't demand, but appeals; he doesn't abolish slavery outright but models a new way of relating that undermines its very foundation. Onesimus, once a runaway slave, is now a "useful" brother, transformed by Christ. This letter challenges us to consider how the Gospel should truly transform *our* relationships, with those who have wronged us, those different from us, or those we might perceive as "lesser." It calls us to extend forgiveness, practice reconciliation, and see every person through the eyes of Christ, recognizing their inherent dignity and potential as fellow image-bearers of God.

This week, as you read Philemon, reflect on a relationship in your life that needs grace, forgiveness, or reconciliation. How can the principles modeled in this letter guide your actions and attitudes? How does seeing someone "in Christ" change how you treat them?

Key Scriptures:

- **Philemon 1-3:** Greetings and Prayer of Thanksgiving for Philemon
- **Philemon 4-7:** Philemon's Love and Faith
- **Philemon 8-16:** Paul's Appeal for Onesimus
- **Philemon 17-22:** Paul's Promise to Pay and Confidence in Philemon
- **Philemon 23-25:** Final Greetings

Reflection Questions:

1. Paul could have commanded Philemon, but instead, he appeals to him. What does this approach teach us about persuasion, love, and leadership in Christian relationships?

2. How does the transformation of Onesimus (from "useless" to "useful" and "beloved brother") illustrate the power of the Gospel to change individuals and their relationships?

3. The letter to Philemon, though not directly abolishing slavery, profoundly undermines its principles. How does the concept of "brotherhood/sisterhood in Christ" challenge societal norms and hierarchies?

4. Paul offers to pay Philemon for any wrong Onesimus committed. What does this reveal about Paul's character and the nature of reconciliation? How might this principle apply in our lives?

5. What practical lessons can you take from this short letter about extending forgiveness, seeking reconciliation, and demonstrating the love of Christ in your daily life?

Week 39 Workbook

Date: _____

Key Takeaways from Devotional Thought:

_____

_____

_____

_____

_____

Insights from Philemon:

_____

_____

_____

_____

Devotional Reflection: What insights on forgiveness did you gain from God's Word this week?

_____

_____

_____

_____

_____

_____

_____

_____

_____

Week 40: Justification by Faith: The Core of Paul's Gospel

Having systematically journeyed through Paul's individual epistles, from his comprehensive theological treatise in Romans to his personal appeal in Philemon, we now begin a series of "Deeper Dives into Key Pauline Themes." This week, we focus on the foundational doctrine that underpins Paul's entire message: **Justification by Faith**. This is the beating heart of the Gospel Paul preached, the radical truth that sets Christianity apart, and the liberating answer to humanity's greatest dilemma.

Paul relentlessly argues that humanity, universally tainted by sin, cannot earn God's favor or salvation through adherence to the Law or good works. Instead, God, in His boundless grace, has provided a means for sinful humanity to be declared righteous in His sight. This declaration, or "justification," is not based on our merit but on the perfect obedience and sacrificial death of Jesus Christ. It is received as a pure gift, solely through **faith** in Him. We will explore how Paul consistently presents this truth, primarily from Romans and Galatians, emphasizing its implications for our standing before God, our freedom from the Law's condemnation, and the very nature of salvation.

Understanding justification by faith is not just theological knowledge; it is the cornerstone of our peace with God and the foundation of our spiritual security.

Devotional Thought: The Immeasurable Gift of Righteousness

Imagine standing before a perfectly holy and just God, knowing your countless imperfections and failures. What could possibly make you acceptable? Paul's answer, central to his Gospel, is **justification by faith**. It is the breathtaking truth that God, out of His sheer grace, imputes Christ's perfect righteousness to us when we believe. We are not just forgiven; we are declared "not guilty," and more profoundly, "righteous" in Christ. This profound act changes our legal standing before

God from condemned sinner to righteous son or daughter. It means that our striving, our attempts to earn favor, and our fear of not being good enough are all rendered powerless in the face of God's overwhelming grace. This week, as you meditate on "justification by faith," allow this truth to wash over you. How does understanding that your righteousness is a gift, not an achievement, bring you peace and security? How does it deepen your gratitude for Christ's sacrifice? Let this core truth free you to live not *for* approval, but *from* acceptance, resting in the immeasurable gift of God's perfect righteousness in Christ.

Key Scriptures:

- **Romans 3:21-26:** Righteousness Through Faith in Christ

- **Romans 4:1-8:** Abraham Justified by Faith

- **Romans 5:1-2:** Peace with God Through Justification by Faith

- **Romans 5:12-19:** Adam and Christ: Righteousness Through One Act of Obedience

- **Romans 10:9-10:** Confession and Belief Lead to Righteousness and Salvation

- **Galatians 2:15-21:** Justification Not by Works of the Law

- **Galatians 3:6-14:** Abraham's Faith and the Curse of the Law

- **Ephesians 2:8-9:** Salvation by Grace Through Faith, Not by Works

- **Philippians 3:7-9:** Paul's Renunciation of Righteousness from the Law

Reflection Questions:

1. In what ways did Paul consistently contrast justification by faith with justification by works of the Law? What fundamental differences does he highlight?

2. Romans 5:1 states, "Therefore, since we have been justified by faith, we have peace with God through our Lord Jesus Christ." How does understanding your justification impact your relationship with God and your inner peace?

3. Why is the example of Abraham so crucial to Paul's argument for justification by faith in Romans 4 and Galatians 3?

4. Paul emphasizes that "the righteous will live by faith" (Romans 1:17, Galatians 3:11). What does it mean to *live* by faith, beyond merely being *justified* by faith?

5. How does the doctrine of justification by faith protect against both legalism (trying to earn salvation) and antinomianism (living without regard for God's law because grace abounds)?

Week 40 Workbook

Date: _____

Key Takeaways from Devotional Thought:

_____

_____

_____

_____

Insights from this week's Bible study:

_____

_____

_____

_____

Devotional Reflection: What did you learn about faith from God's Word this week?

_____

_____

_____

_____

_____

_____

Week 41: Life in the Spirit: Paul on Sanctification and Empowerment

Having explored the pivotal doctrine of justification by faith, we now turn to another transformative theme central to Paul's theology: **Life in the Spirit, encompassing sanctification and empowerment**. For Paul, salvation is not merely a legal declaration; it is a dynamic, ongoing transformation powered by the indwelling Holy Spirit. This week, we will delve into how Paul describes the Spirit's vital role in the believer's life, moving them from spiritual death to new life, empowering them to overcome sin, grow in Christ-likeness, and live out their faith with divine strength.

Paul presents the Holy Spirit not as an abstract concept, but as a real, active Person of the Godhead who dwells within every believer from the moment of conversion. The Spirit provides the power for sanctification, the process of becoming more like Christ ,and enables believers to put to death the deeds of the flesh and live in obedience to God's will.

Beyond moral transformation, the Spirit also **empowers** believers for witness, worship, and service, gifting them for the building up of the church. We will draw primarily from Romans 8, Galatians 5, and passages in 1 Corinthians and Ephesians to understand this glorious reality of Spirit-filled living.

Devotional Thought: Walking in the Spirit, Living in Power

One of Paul's most profound truths is that because we are justified by faith, we are now free to **walk in the Spirit** (Galatians 5:16). This means we are no longer enslaved to sin or the Law, but are led by the Spirit, who empowers us to live lives pleasing to God. Romans 8 is a cornerstone, declaring "there is now no condemnation for those who are in Christ Jesus" because "the law of the Spirit of life has set you free in Christ Jesus from the law of sin and death" (Romans 8:1-2).

This is an active, daily reliance on the Spirit's power to guide our thoughts, desires, and actions. The Spirit produces His fruit in us, love, joy, peace, patience, kindness, goodness, faithfulness, gentleness, self-control, and equips us with spiritual gifts for ministry. This week, reflect on the presence of the Holy Spirit in your life. Are you consciously relying on His power for sanctification and guidance? How can you more fully yield to His leading, allowing Him to produce His fruit and empower your walk with Christ?

Key Scriptures:

- **Romans 8:1-17:** No Condemnation, Life in the Spirit
- **Romans 8:26-27:** The Spirit Helps Us in Our Weakness
- **Romans 12:6-8:** Gifts of Grace (general mention related to Spirit's work)
- **Galatians 5:16-26:** Walk by the Spirit; Fruit of the Spirit vs. Works of the Flesh
- **Ephesians 1:13-14:** Sealed with the Holy Spirit of Promise
- **Ephesians 3:14-19:** Strengthened with Power Through His Spirit
- **Ephesians 4:30:** Do Not Grieve the Holy Spirit
- **1 Corinthians 2:10-16:** The Spirit Reveals God's Wisdom
- **1 Corinthians 12:4-11:** Diversity of Spiritual Gifts, One Spirit
- **2 Corinthians 3:17-18:** The Lord is the Spirit, and Where the Spirit of the Lord is, There is Freedom; Being Transformed

Reflection Questions:

1. How does Paul describe the freedom and new identity believers have by "life in the Spirit" in Romans 8? What are the practical implications of this freedom?

2. Galatians 5 contrasts the "works of the flesh" with the "fruit of the Spirit." What is the significance of the Spirit producing "fruit" in us, rather than us simply trying to produce good "works"?

3. According to Paul, what is the role of the Holy Spirit in guiding and helping believers in their walk with God (e.g., Romans 8:26-27)?

4. How do 1 Corinthians 12 and Ephesians 4 describe the Spirit's empowerment of believers for service within the church? Why is diversity of gifts essential?

5. What does it mean to "walk by the Spirit" (Galatians 5:16)? What does this look like in your daily life, and what steps can you take to cultivate a greater reliance on the Spirit?

Week 41 Workbook

Date: _____

Key Takeaways from Devotional Thought:

_____

_____

_____

_____

_____

Insights from this week's Bible study:

_____

_____

_____

_____

_____

Devotional Reflection: How did this week's study deepen your understanding of Spirit-filled living?

_____

_____

_____

_____

_____

_____

_____

_____

_____

Week 42: The Church as the Body of Christ: Unity, Diversity, and Mission

Having explored the fundamental truths of **justification by faith** and **life in the Spirit**, we now turn our attention to Paul's profound understanding of the **Church**. For Paul, the Church is not merely a human organization or a building; it is the living **Body of Christ**, a dynamic spiritual organism uniquely united to its head, Jesus Christ.

This week, we will delve into Paul's rich teaching on the nature of the Church, highlighting its essential characteristics: **unity, diversity, and its ultimate mission** in the world.

Paul emphasizes that despite the diverse backgrounds, gifts, and roles of individual believers, they are all intimately connected by the Holy Spirit and form one unified body. This **unity** is not uniformity but a Spirit-given bond that transcends social, ethnic, and economic distinctions. Within this unity, there is incredible **diversity** of spiritual gifts, each essential for the health and growth of the whole. Every member has a vital function, empowered by the same Spirit for the common good.

This unified and diverse body is then called to a specific **mission**: to live out and proclaim the Gospel of Jesus Christ to the world, demonstrating God's wisdom, love, and reconciliation. We will draw from key passages, particularly in 1 Corinthians and Ephesians, to grasp the beauty and power of the Church as Christ's hands and feet on earth.

Devotional Thought: Interconnectedness and Purpose

Paul's analogy of the Church as the **Body of Christ** is one of the most powerful metaphors in the New Testament. It speaks volumes about our identity and purpose as believers. Just as a physical body has many different parts, each with its own function, so too does the Church. No part is insignificant, and every part is essential for the healthy functioning of the whole (1 Corinthians 12).

This means there's no room for unhealthy competition, comparison, or isolation within the Church. Instead, we are called to mutual dependence, care, and cooperation. Our unity in Christ breaks down all barriers that divide humanity, fostering a family where love, forgiveness, and service abound. And as a unified body, we have a collective mission to be salt and light in the world, demonstrating the love and truth of Christ. This week, reflect on your place within the Body of Christ.

Do you understand and embrace your unique role and gifts? How can you actively contribute to the unity and mission of your local church, recognizing that when one part suffers, all suffer, and when one part rejoices, all rejoice?

Key Scriptures:

- **Romans 12:3-8:** One Body, Many Members, Different Gifts
- **1 Corinthians 12:12-31:** The Body of Christ, One Spirit, Many Gifts
- **1 Corinthians 14:12, 26-33:** Orderly Use of Gifts for Edification
- **Ephesians 1:22-23:** Christ is the Head of the Church, His Body
- **Ephesians 2:19-22:** Fellow Citizens with Saints, Built on the Foundation
- **Ephesians 4:1-16:** Unity of the Spirit; Gifts for Building Up the Body
- **Colossians 1:18:** Christ is the Head of the Body, the Church
- **Colossians 3:12-17:** Living as God's Chosen People, United in Love

Reflection Questions:

1. What are the key elements of Paul's "Body of Christ" metaphor in 1 Corinthians 12 and Romans 12? How does this metaphor challenge individualism within the Christian faith?

2. Paul emphasizes both unity and diversity within the Church. How are these two concepts balanced, and why is both crucial for a healthy church?

3. According to Ephesians 4:11-16, what is the purpose of spiritual gifts given to the Church? How do these gifts contribute to the Church's growth and maturity?

4. How does Paul describe the Church's identity and function in the world (e.g., Ephesians 3:10, 5:25-27)? What is its ultimate mission?

5. Consider your local church community. How can you personally contribute to fostering greater unity, valuing diversity of gifts, and actively participating in its mission?

Week 42 Workbook

Date: _____

Key Takeaways from Devotional Thought:

_____

_____

_____

_____

Insights from this week's Bible study:

_____

_____

_____

_____

Devotional Reflection: How did this week's study deepen your understanding of what it means to be a believer?

_____

_____

_____

_____

_____

_____

Week 43: Practical Godliness: Ethics for the Christian Life

Having explored foundational doctrines like justification by faith, the transformative power of the Holy Spirit, and the nature of the Church, we now turn to a theme woven throughout all of Paul's epistles: **Practical Godliness**. For Paul, true Christian faith is never abstract or theoretical; it always leads to tangible transformation in behavior, relationships, and daily conduct. This week, we will delve into Paul's ethical teachings, understanding that our salvation in Christ calls us to a new way of living that reflects God's character and glorifies Him in every sphere of life.

Paul consistently moves from profound theological truth to practical application. His letters are replete with exhortations on how believers should live, both individually and corporately. He addresses a wide array of ethical topics, including sexual purity, honesty, integrity in work, healthy relationships within families and the church, resolving conflict, and living with love and humility towards all. For Paul, **Christian ethics are rooted in our new identity in Christ and empowered by the Holy Spirit.**

Our behavior is not merely about following rules, but about expressing the reality of who we have become in Christ – a new creation. We will draw from a variety of Paul's letters, including Romans, Ephesians, Colossians, and the Pastoral Epistles, to understand the comprehensive nature of Paul's call to practical godliness.

Devotional Thought: Living a Life Worthy of the Calling

Paul's teaching on practical godliness can be summarized by his repeated call to "walk worthy" of the calling we have received (Ephesians 4:1). What does this mean? It means our daily lives should align with the incredible grace and truth we have embraced. If we are justified by faith, then legalism has no hold on us, and we are free to live by the Spirit. If we are members of Christ's body, then we are called to love and serve one another. Paul provides clear, actionable guidance on how this looks in concrete situations: putting off anger, speaking truth, working diligently, being kind and forgiving, submitting to one another out of reverence for Christ, and living with self-control.

This week, as you reflect on Paul's ethical teachings, consider one area of your life where you can intentionally "put off" an old habit or attitude and "put on" a new, godly one. How can your daily actions better reflect the truth of who you are in Christ and the calling God has placed on your life?

Key Scriptures:

- **Romans 6:1-14:** Dead to Sin, Alive to God

- **Romans 12:1-2:** Present Your Bodies as a Living Sacrifice; Transformed by the Renewal of Your Mind

- **Romans 13:8-10:** Love Fulfills the Law

- **Ephesians 4:17-32:** Put Off the Old Self, Put On the New Self (Practical Exhortations)

- **Ephesians 5:1-7:** Imitate God, Walk in Love

- **Ephesians 5:15-21:** Walk as Wise, Filled with the Spirit

- **Ephesians 5:22-6:9:** Household Codes (Wives/Husbands, Children/Parents, Slaves/Masters)

- **Colossians 3:1-11:** Set Your Minds on Things Above; Put Off the Old, Put On the New

- **Colossians 3:12-17:** Clothes of the New Self (Compassion, Kindness, Humility, etc.)

- **1 Thessalonians 4:3-8:** God's Will is Your Sanctification (Sexual Purity)

- **Titus 2:11-14:** The Grace of God Teaches Us to Live Godly Lives

- **Philippians 4:8-9:** Whatever is True, Noble, Right, Pure, Lovely, Admirable

Reflection Questions:

1. How does Paul connect our new identity in Christ (e.g., "dead to sin," "new creation") to our call to live a godly life?

2. What does it mean to "present your bodies as a living sacrifice" and to be "transformed by the renewal of your mind" as described in Romans 12:1-2? How can you live this out daily?

3. Paul often uses the language of "putting off" the old self and "putting on" the new self (Ephesians 4, Colossians 3). What specific attitudes or behaviors does he tell us to put off, and what should we put on instead?

4. How do Paul's "household codes" (Ephesians 5-6, Colossians 3) apply to modern relationships within families, workplaces, and communities? What underlying principles remain timeless?

5. Based on these passages, what are 2-3 practical changes you can implement this week to better demonstrate practical godliness in your life?

Week 43 Workbook

Date: _____

Key Takeaways from Devotional Thought:

_____

_____

_____

_____

_____

Insights from this week's Bible study:

_____

_____

_____

_____

_____

Devotional Reflection: How did this week's study deepen your understanding of Christian ethics?

_____

_____

_____

_____

_____

_____

_____

_____

_____

_____

Week 44: Eschatology and Hope: Paul on Christ's Return and the New Creation

As we near the conclusion of our "Deeper Dives into Key Pauline Themes," this week we focus on **Eschatology and Hope: Paul on Christ's Return and the New Creation**. Throughout his letters, Paul consistently points believers to the future hope rooted in the glorious return of Jesus Christ and the ultimate renewal of all things. This future reality is not just a distant event; it profoundly shapes the present life of every Christian.

Paul's eschatology (the study of end times) is highly practical. He addresses topics such as the resurrection of believers, the transformation of creation, the judgment seat of Christ, and the ultimate victory of God's plan. He uses these future truths to comfort the grieving, encourage perseverance in suffering, motivate holy living, and inspire eager expectation. From his earliest letters (1 & 2 Thessalonians) addressing immediate concerns about Christ's coming, to Romans and 1 Corinthians where he expands on the resurrection and the groaning of creation, Paul paints a comprehensive picture of the believer's enduring hope.

This week, we will explore how Paul's teaching on the future empowers our present faith and provides an unshakable foundation for our hope in a world filled with uncertainty.

Devotional Thought: Living with a Future Hope

Paul offers a steadfast and glorious hope: the return of Jesus Christ and the promise of a new creation. This is not wishful thinking but a confident expectation rooted in God's faithfulness and Christ's resurrection. Paul assures us that our labor in the Lord is not in vain, that our sufferings are temporary, and that our bodies will be resurrected in glory.

This future hope is meant to transform our present reality. It comforts us when we grieve, motivates us to live holy lives, gives us strength to endure persecution, and directs our focus away from earthly perishable things towards eternal, imperishable realities.

Knowing that Christ will return and make all things new provides an anchor for our souls. This week, as you reflect on Paul's eschatological teachings, how does the hope of Christ's return and the new creation impact your daily perspective? How can you cultivate a more profound and resilient hope, allowing it to shape your priorities and bring comfort amidst life's challenges?

Key Scriptures:

- **1 Thessalonians 4:13-18:** The Comfort of Christ's Return and the Resurrection

- **1 Thessalonians 5:1-11:** The Day of the Lord: Living Alert and Soberly

- **2 Thessalonians 1:5-10:** God's Righteous Judgment at Christ's Coming

- **2 Thessalonians 2:1-12:** The Man of Lawlessness and the Day of the Lord

- **Romans 8:18-25:** The Groaning Creation and Our Future Hope

- **Romans 13:11-14:** Salvation is Nearer; Put on Christ

- **1 Corinthians 15:12-58:** The Resurrection of the Dead and Our Glorified Bodies

- **Philippians 3:20-21:** Our Citizenship is in Heaven; Christ Will Transform Our Lowly Bodies

- **Colossians 3:1-4:** Set Your Minds on Things Above; Your Life is Hidden with Christ

Reflection Questions:

1. What comfort does Paul offer in 1 Thessalonians 4:13-18 regarding those who have died in Christ? How does this passage address common fears or misunderstandings about death?

2. How does Paul use the "Day of the Lord" in 1 & 2 Thessalonians to motivate both vigilance and hope among believers?

3. In Romans 8:18-25, Paul describes creation groaning for redemption. What does this teach us about God's ultimate plan for both humanity and the physical world?

4. Why is the resurrection of Christ and the future resurrection of believers so central to Paul's Gospel, as detailed in 1 Corinthians 15? What are the implications if there is no resurrection?

5. How should our future hope in Christ's return and the new creation influence our current priorities, ethical choices, and perseverance in faith?

Week 44 Workbook

Date: _____

Key Takeaways from Devotional Thought:

_____

_____

_____

_____

_____

Insights from this week's Bible study:

_____

_____

_____

_____

_____

Devotional Reflection: How did this week's study deepen your understanding of Christian hope?

_____

_____

_____

_____

_____

_____

_____

_____

_____

Part 9: The General Epistles

We've just completed our extensive journey through the Pauline Epistles, gaining a deep understanding of Paul's foundational theological truths and their practical implications for Christian living. Now, we shift our focus to **Part 9: The General Epistles**.

These letters, also known as the Catholic Epistles (meaning "universal" or "general" because they weren't primarily addressed to specific churches), offer diverse perspectives and crucial exhortations for believers facing various challenges and temptations.

While Paul's letters often lay out systematic theology, the General Epistles frequently serve as robust pastoral guides, emphasizing perseverance in faith, the importance of genuine works as evidence of faith, warnings against false teaching, and encouragement in suffering. They broaden our understanding of the early church's struggles and triumphs, providing timeless wisdom for Christians in every age.

Over the next few weeks, we'll dive into Hebrews, James, Peter, John, and Jude, each offering unique insights into the Christian walk.

Week 45: Hebrews – The Superiority of Christ

As we begin our exploration of the General Epistles, we open with the profound and perhaps most unique book in this collection: **Hebrews**. Unlike Paul's letters, the author of Hebrews is not explicitly named, but its message is undeniably powerful and central to Christian doctrine. Written to a community of Jewish believers who were likely facing persecution and temptation to revert to Judaism, Hebrews presents a compelling argument for the **absolute superiority of Jesus Christ** over every aspect of the Old Covenant.

The author systematically demonstrates that Jesus is greater than angels, Moses, the Levitical priesthood, and the Old Covenant sacrifices. He is the ultimate High Priest, offering a perfect, once-for-all sacrifice that truly atones for sin and grants direct access to God. Hebrews calls its readers to hold fast to their confession, to persevere in faith, and to draw near to God with confidence, seeing Jesus as the supreme revelation of God and the ultimate fulfillment of God's promises. This letter is a masterful theological treatise, urging steadfastness and maturity in the Christian faith.

Devotional Thought: Looking to Jesus, the Author and Perfecter of Our Faith

The central message of Hebrews is simple: **Jesus is better.** He is the ultimate, the final, the complete. In a world full of shifting foundations and competing loyalties, Hebrews anchors us to the unchanging supremacy of

Christ. It confronts any tendency to regress in our faith or seek comfort in lesser things. The author urges us to "fix our eyes on Jesus, the author and perfecter of our faith" (Hebrews 12:2), because He has accomplished all that is necessary for our salvation and perseverance. His sacrifice is sufficient, His priesthood eternal, and His covenant superior.

This week, consider what "lesser things" might be vying for your attention or tempting you to waver in your commitment to Christ. How does understanding Jesus' unparalleled superiority strengthen your resolve to draw near to God with confidence and run the race of faith with endurance? Let the truths of Hebrews deepen your appreciation for Christ and fortify your faith.

Key Scriptures:

- **Hebrews 1:1-4:** God's Final Word in His Son, Superior to Angels
- **Hebrews 2:1-4:** The Danger of Neglecting Salvation
- **Hebrews 3:1-6:** Jesus is Greater Than Moses
- **Hebrews 4:14-16:** Jesus, Our Great High Priest, and Boldness to Approach the Throne of Grace
- **Hebrews 7:11-28:** Jesus, a Priest Like Melchizedek, a Superior Priesthood
- **Hebrews 8:6-13:** Jesus, the Mediator of a Better Covenant
- **Hebrews 9:11-14:** Christ's Superior Sacrifice
- **Hebrews 10:19-25:** Full Assurance of Faith and Perseverance
- **Hebrews 11:1-40:** The Nature of Faith and Examples from History
- **Hebrews 12:1-3:** Running the Race with Perseverance, Fixing Our Eyes on Jesus
- **Hebrews 13:8:** Jesus Christ is the Same Yesterday, Today, and Forever

Reflection Questions:

1. How does the author of Hebrews demonstrate Jesus' superiority over angels and Moses? What is the significance of these comparisons for the original audience and for us today?
2. What does Hebrews teach about Jesus as our High Priest (e.g., Hebrews 4:14-16, 7:23-28)? How does His priesthood differ from the Levitical priesthood, and what confidence does this give us?

3. The letter repeatedly warns against "drifting away" or "falling away." What specific dangers or temptations was the audience facing, and what are contemporary parallels?

4. Hebrews 11 is often called the "Hall of Faith." What common thread runs through the examples of faith, and how do they encourage perseverance?

5. Based on Hebrews 12:1-3, what does it mean to "run with endurance" the race set before us, and how is "fixing our eyes on Jesus" essential to this?

Week 45 Workbook

Date: _____

Key Takeaways from Devotional Thought:

_____
_____
_____
_____

Insights from Hebrews:

_____
_____
_____
_____

Devotional Reflection: How did this week's study deepen your understanding of maturity in Christian faith?

_____
_____
_____
_____
_____
_____
_____
_____
_____

Week 46: James – Faith in Action: Living Out Your Beliefs

Continuing our study of the General Epistles, this week we turn to the book of **James**. Often called the "Proverbs of the New Testament" due to its practical, wisdom-oriented instruction, this letter was likely written by James, the half-brother of Jesus and a prominent leader in the early Jerusalem church. Addressed to "the twelve tribes scattered among the nations" (James 1:1), it offers timeless counsel to Jewish Christians facing trials, temptations, and practical challenges in their faith walk.

James's central theme is the inseparable link between genuine faith and righteous living. He confronts nominal Christianity directly, famously declaring that "faith without works is dead" (James 2:26). This is not a contradiction of Paul's doctrine of justification by faith, but rather a complementary emphasis: true faith, the kind that saves, *always* produces evidence in changed lives and good works.

James challenges believers to demonstrate their faith through perseverance in trials, control of the tongue, resisting temptation, humility, impartial treatment of others, and caring for the vulnerable. It's a powerful call to integrity, sincerity, and tangible obedience that validates one's profession of faith.

Devotional Thought: The Evidence of a Living Faith

James's letter can feel confrontational precisely because it holds up a mirror to our lives and asks, "What does your faith *look* like?" In a world that often values outward profession over inward transformation, James reminds us that genuine faith is not passive intellectual ascent but active, living trust that expresses itself in our choices, words, and deeds.

The "works" James speaks of are not a means to earn salvation, but the natural, unavoidable fruit of a heart truly transformed by God's grace. When we face trials, do we seek wisdom from God? When we speak, do our words build up or tear down? When we see someone in need, do we simply offer empty words or do we extend practical help?

This week, let the direct challenge of James inspire you. How does your faith manifest itself in your daily life, your relationships, and your responses to the world around you? What "works" are truly evident as a result of your living faith in Christ?

Key Scriptures:

- **James 1:2-4:** Perseverance in Trials
- **James 1:5-8:** Asking for Wisdom in Faith
- **James 1:12-16:** Resisting Temptation
- **James 1:19-27:** Hearing and Doing the Word; True Religion
- **James 2:1-13:** Impartiality and the Royal Law
- **James 2:14-26:** Faith Without Works Is Dead
- **James 3:1-12:** Taming the Tongue
- **James 3:13-18:** Two Kinds of Wisdom (Earthly vs. Heavenly)
- **James 4:1-10:** Humility Before God; Resist the Devil
- **James 4:11-17:** Avoiding Slander and Boasting; God's Will
- **James 5:1-6:** Warning to the Rich
- **James 5:7-12:** Patience in Suffering
- **James 5:13-18:** Prayer for the Sick; Power of Righteous Prayer

Reflection Questions:

1. How does James's teaching on perseverance in trials (James 1:2-4) encourage a different perspective on difficulties than a purely secular one?

2. What is the main point James is making in James 2:14-26 regarding faith and works? How does this passage complement rather than contradict Paul's teaching on justification by faith?

3. Why does James place such a strong emphasis on controlling the tongue in James 3:1-12? What are the dangers of an uncontrolled tongue?

4. James defines "pure and faultless religion" in James 1:27. What are the two key components he highlights, and what do they tell us about practical godliness?

5. What practical steps can you take this week to apply James's call to impartial love, wise speech, and humble submission to God in your daily life?

Week 46 Workbook

Date: _____

Key Takeaways from Devotional Thought:

_____
_____
_____
_____
_____

Insights from James:

_____
_____
_____
_____

Devotional Reflection: What Biblical insights on integrity did you gain this week?

_____
_____
_____
_____
_____
_____
_____
_____

Week 47: 1 & 2 Peter – Hope, Holiness, and Suffering for Christ

This week, we delve into the two epistles written by the Apostle Peter: **1 Peter and 2 Peter**. These letters offer vital guidance to believers grappling with persecution, false teaching, and the call to live out their faith amidst a hostile world. Peter, a prominent figure in the early church and one of Jesus' closest disciples, writes with a pastoral heart, strengthening and challenging his readers.

1 Peter is primarily a message of **hope and encouragement amidst suffering.** Written to scattered believers facing various forms of trials and hostility, Peter reminds them of their new identity in Christ, chosen, holy, and set apart. He emphasizes that suffering for Christ is not a sign of God's displeasure but an expected part of the Christian life that refines faith and prepares believers for future glory. The letter calls for holy living, respectful submission in various relationships, and confident witness to the Gospel, even when it costs them.

2 Peter, on the other hand, is a powerful warning against **false teachers** and a fervent call to **spiritual growth and steadfastness** in light of Christ's certain return. Peter urges believers to grow in knowledge of Christ, to be diligent in their faith, and to guard against deceptive doctrines that undermine truth and promote immorality. He reaffirms the certainty of Christ's second coming and the new heavens and new earth, using this future hope as a strong motivation for righteous living and holy conduct.

Devotional Thought: Anchored in Hope, Refined by Fire

Peter's epistles speak powerfully to a central tension of the Christian life: living with **hope in glory** while enduring **suffering in the present.** He teaches us that our hope isn't a passive waiting, but an active, living expectation rooted in Christ's resurrection. This hope empowers us to embrace a life of holiness, knowing that we are called to be set apart for God's purposes. When trials come, Peter reminds us that they are part of God's refining process, testing our faith and producing perseverance. In an age where truth is often diluted or distorted, Peter's second letter also calls us to diligent growth in our knowledge of God and His Word, so we can discern truth from error and stand firm.

This week, reflect on your own approach to suffering and the pursuit of holiness. How can the living hope we have in Christ transform your perspective on challenges? In what ways are you actively growing in your faith to stand firm against deception and live a life that honors God?

Key Scriptures:

- **1 Peter 1:3-9:** A Living Hope Through Resurrection, Tested by Suffering
- **1 Peter 1:13-16:** Be Holy, Because I Am Holy
- **1 Peter 2:1-5:** Living Stones, a Spiritual House
- **1 Peter 2:9-12:** A Chosen Race, a Holy Nation; Live Honorably Among the Gentiles
- **1 Peter 3:13-17:** Suffering for Righteousness' Sake; Be Prepared to Give an Answer
- **1 Peter 4:12-19:** Suffering for Christ's Name
- **1 Peter 5:6-11:** Humble Yourselves, Resist the Devil, God Will Restore
- **2 Peter 1:3-11:** God's Divine Power and Growth in Godliness
- **2 Peter 2:1-3:** Warning Against False Teachers
- **2 Peter 3:3-14:** The Certainty of Christ's Coming and the New Heavens/New Earth

Reflection Questions:

1. How does Peter's concept of a "living hope" (1 Peter 1:3) contrast with a worldly understanding of hope? What is this hope based on?

2. What is the purpose of suffering for the Christian, according to 1 Peter? How can embracing this perspective change your response to trials?

3. In 1 Peter 2:9-10, Peter describes believers as a "chosen race, a royal priesthood, a holy nation." What implications does this identity have for how Christians should live in the world?

4. Why does Peter dedicate significant space in 2 Peter to warning against false teachers? What characteristics of false teaching does he highlight, and how can believers protect themselves?

5. How does the certainty of Christ's return and the promise of new heavens and new earth (2 Peter 3) serve as a motivation for holy living and spiritual diligence in the present?

Week 47 Workbook

Date: _____

Key Takeaways from Devotional Thought:

_____

_____

_____

_____

_____

Insights from 1&2 Peter:

_____

_____

_____

_____

_____

Devotional Reflection: How did this week's study deepen your understanding of spiritual growth?

_____

_____

_____

_____

_____

_____

_____

_____

_____

Week 48: 1, 2, & 3 John – Love, Truth, and Fellowship

This week, we turn to the three short, incredibly profound, epistles of **1, 2, and 3 John.** These letters, written by the Apostle John, the "beloved disciple," are distinct from his Gospel but share common themes and vocabulary, emphasizing the core tenets of Christian life: **love, truth, and fellowship with God and one another.** They were likely written to combat early Gnostic heresies that denied the true humanity of Christ and to address divisions within Christian communities.

1 John is arguably the most comprehensive of the three. It serves as a test of genuine faith, outlining characteristics that demonstrate true fellowship with God: walking in the light, confessing sin, obeying God's commands (especially the command to love one another), and holding to the truth of Jesus Christ's humanity and divinity. It provides assurance to believers who genuinely walk with God and warns against those who deny Christ or live in deliberate sin.

2 John is a brief but pointed letter addressed to "the chosen lady and her children" (likely a church and its members). It emphasizes the importance of **walking in truth and love**, and crucially, warns against extending hospitality to false teachers. It calls for discernment and steadfastness in sound doctrine.

3 John is a personal letter to a faithful believer named Gaius. It commends Gaius for his hospitality to traveling missionaries ("walking in truth") and expresses concern about a leader named Diotrephes, who was exhibiting pride and a lack of love. This letter provides a glimpse into the practical challenges and interpersonal dynamics within early Christian communities, underscoring the importance of humble service and genuine fellowship.

Together, these letters from John serve as a timeless reminder that true faith is not just intellectual assent, but a transformative relationship with God that manifests in genuine love for one another and unwavering adherence to the truth of Jesus Christ.

Devotional Thought: The Intertwined Dance of Love and Truth

John's letters beautifully highlight that authentic Christianity is a seamless blend of **love and truth.** You cannot truly love God if you deny His truth, and you cannot truly claim to know truth if you do not walk in love. 1 John asserts that "God is love," but also that "God is light" – meaning He is pure truth and holiness. Living in fellowship with Him means walking in both. This has profound implications for our relationships within the church and our witness to the world. We are called to love one another deeply, sacrificially, and practically, just as Christ loved us.

This love must be grounded in the unwavering truth of the Gospel, discerning error and standing firm against anything that distorts who Jesus is or what He has done. This week, examine your own life: where might you be tempted to compromise truth for the sake of perceived "love," or, conversely, to uphold truth without genuine love? How can you cultivate a deeper commitment to both, recognizing that they are inextricably linked in the heart of God and the practice of true faith?

Key Scriptures:

- **1 John 1:5-10:** God is Light; Walking in Light and Confessing Sin
- **1 John 2:3-6:** Obedience as Evidence of Knowing God
- **1 John 2:15-17:** Do Not Love the World
- **1 John 3:1-3:** Children of God; Our Future Hope
- **1 John 3:16-18:** Love in Action
- **1 John 4:7-12:** God Is Love; Love One Another
- **1 John 4:13-21:** God's Love Made Perfect in Us; Love for God and Neighbor
- **1 John 5:1-5:** Victory Over the World Through Faith

- **1 John 5:13:** Assurance of Salvation
- **2 John 1:4-6:** Walking in Truth and Love
- **2 John 1:7-11:** Warning Against False Teachers and Not Supporting Them
- **3 John 1:3-4:** Gaius's Faithfulness and Walking in Truth
- **3 John 1:9-11:** Diotrephes and Demetrius

Reflection Questions:

1. According to 1 John, what are the primary "tests" or evidence of genuine fellowship with God? How do these tests challenge mere intellectual belief?

2. How does John define "love" in his letters, particularly in 1 John 4:7-12 and 1 John 3:16-18? What does this mean for how believers should interact with each other?

3. Why is acknowledging Jesus' true humanity and divinity ("Christ has come in the flesh") so crucial for John, especially in 1 John and 2 John? What kind of false teaching was he combating?

4. What practical lessons can be drawn from 2 John regarding discerning false teachers and upholding biblical truth within the church?

5. What can we learn from the contrasts between Gaius and Diotrephes in 3 John about Christian leadership, hospitality, and humility?

Week 48 Workbook

Date: _____

Key Takeaways from Devotional Thought:

_____

_____

_____

_____

_____

Insights from 1, 2 and 3 John:

_____

_____

_____

_____

_____

Devotional Reflection: How did this week's study deepen your understanding of walking in truth and love?

_____

_____

_____

_____

_____

_____

_____

_____

_____

_____

Week 49: Jude – Contending for the Faith

This week, we engage with the powerful and concise book of **Jude**. This short letter, likely written by Jude (Judas), the brother of James and half-brother of Jesus, serves as an urgent and passionate call to **contend earnestly for the faith** that was once for all delivered to the saints (Jude 3). Addressed to all believers, it confronts the insidious threat of false teachers who had infiltrated the church, distorting the grace of God and promoting immorality.

Jude pulls no punches, describing these ungodly individuals and their deceptive practices in vivid detail. He warns believers by drawing on historical examples of rebellion and judgment from both Old Testament and extra-biblical sources. His primary purpose is to arm believers with discernment and encourage them to stand firm against apostasy.

Rather than simply exposing error, Jude also provides practical instructions for how genuine believers should respond: by building themselves up in their most holy faith, praying in the Holy Spirit, keeping themselves in God's love, and showing mercy to those who waver. Jude is a timeless reminder of the need for vigilance, theological clarity, and unwavering commitment to the truth of the Gospel.

Devotional Thought: Guardians of the Truth

Jude's letter is a wake-up call for every generation of believers. It reminds us that spiritual complacency can be dangerous, especially when truth is under attack from within. The call to **"contend earnestly for the**

faith" is not an invitation to argue aggressively, but a charge to passionately defend the core truths of the Gospel against distortion and compromise. It requires knowing what we believe, why we believe it, and how to spot genuine teaching versus deceptive error. Jude also balances this warning with a profound encouragement to actively pursue our own spiritual growth, by building ourselves up in the faith and staying rooted in God's love.

This week, consider the truths of the Gospel that are most precious to you. How are you actively protecting and proclaiming these truths in your life and community? In what ways can you better build yourself up in your faith, so you are equipped to stand firm and discern what is true in a world often filled with deceptive voices?

Key Scriptures:

- **Jude 1-3:** Greeting and Exhortation to Contend for the Faith
- **Jude 4:** The Danger of Ungodly Intruders
- **Jude 5-7:** Historical Examples of Rebellion and Judgment (Israel, Angels, Sodom and Gomorrah)
- **Jude 8-10:** Denunciation of False Teachers' Character
- **Jude 11-16:** Further Examples and Descriptions of the Ungodly
- **Jude 17-19:** Remembering the Apostles' Warnings
- **Jude 20-23:** Building Yourselves Up in the Faith, Keeping in God's Love, Showing Mercy
- **Jude 24-25:** Doxology: God's Power to Keep Us from Stumbling

Reflection Questions:

1. What does Jude mean by "contending earnestly for the faith" (Jude 3)? What actions might this involve in a modern context?

2. How does Jude use historical examples (e.g., Israel in the wilderness, fallen angels, Sodom and Gomorrah) to warn his readers about the consequences of rebellion and immorality?

3. What specific characteristics of the "ungodly people" does Jude highlight (Jude 4, 8, 12-16)? How can we recognize similar patterns today?

4. Beyond warning, Jude also provides positive instructions for believers in Jude 20-23. What are these instructions, and why are they crucial for spiritual resilience?

5. The doxology in Jude 24-25 emphasizes God's ability to "keep you from stumbling." How does this final affirmation of God's power provide comfort and assurance in the face of spiritual threats?

Week 49 Workbook

Date: _____

Key Takeaways from Devotional Thought:

_____

_____

_____

_____

_____

Insights from Jude:

_____

_____

_____

_____

Devotional Reflection: How did this week's study deepen your understanding of vigilance?

_____

_____

_____

_____

_____

_____

_____

_____

Week 50: The Call to Authentic Faith

This week, we will focus on the **Call to Authentic Faith**, a theme resonating throughout the General Epistles. These letters consistently challenge the notion of a passive, intellectual faith, urging believers to demonstrate their commitment to Christ through tangible actions and transformed lives.

James's emphasis on "faith without works is dead" (James 2:26) is perhaps the most direct expression of this theme. He insists that genuine faith produces fruit in good works, not as a means of earning salvation, but as the natural outflow of a changed heart. 1 John echoes this, urging believers to walk in the light, keep God's commands, and love one another (1 John 1:5-7, 1 John 2:3-6, 1 John 4:7-12). Peter calls believers to a life of holiness (1 Peter 1:15-16), and Jude exhorts them to contend earnestly for the faith (Jude 3). Hebrews, while focusing on Christ's supremacy, also emphasizes perseverance and faithfulness (Hebrews 3:6, 10:35-39).

Together, these letters paint a picture of a dynamic, lived-out faith. It is not simply about what we believe, but how we live. Authentic faith transforms our character, shapes our relationships, and empowers us to endure trials. It is a faith that is both deeply rooted in truth and actively expressed in love.

Devotional Thought: Living What We Believe

The General Epistles invite us to self-examination: does our life reflect the faith we profess? Is there a disconnect between our words and our actions? Authentic faith is not a mere intellectual assent to Christian doctrine, but a radical transformation that touches every aspect of our being. It is a faith that works itself out in love (Galatians 5:6), producing the fruit of the Spirit (Galatians 5:22-23).

This week, consider one area of your life where your actions might not fully align with your beliefs. What practical steps can you take to bridge that gap, allowing your faith to become more visible and tangible in your daily choices? How can you cultivate a more integrated life, where your beliefs are consistently expressed in your behavior, your relationships, and your responses to the world around you?

Key Scriptures:

- **James 2:14-26:** Faith Without Works Is Dead
- **1 John 1:5-7:** Walking in the Light
- **1 John 2:3-6:** Obedience as Evidence of Knowing God
- **1 John 3:16-18:** Love in Action
- **1 John 4:7-12:** God Is Love; Love One Another
- **1 Peter 1:13-16:** Be Holy, Because I Am Holy
- **1 Peter 2:11-12:** Live Honorably Among the Gentiles
- **Hebrews 3:12-14:** Exhort One Another Daily
- **Hebrews 10:24-25:** Stir Up One Another to Love and Good Works
- **Jude 20-21:** Building Yourselves Up in the Faith, Keeping in God's Love

Reflection Questions:

1. How does James's emphasis on "works" complement rather than contradict Paul's teaching on justification by faith?
2. What does it mean to "walk in the light" as described in 1 John 1:5-7? How does this relate to living out an authentic faith?
3. How does the call to love one another (1 John 4:7-12) serve as a demonstration of genuine faith?

4. What practical steps can you take to "live honorably among the Gentiles" (1 Peter 2:12), allowing your life to be a witness to your faith?

5. How can you actively "stir up one another to love and good works" (Hebrews 10:24-25) within your community of believers?

Week 50 Workbook

Date: _____

Key Takeaways from Devotional Thought:

_____

_____

_____

_____

_____

Insights from this week's Bible study:

_____

_____

_____

_____

_____

Devotional Reflection: How did this week's study deepen your understanding of how to live a true Christian life?

_____

_____

_____

_____

_____

_____

_____

_____

_____

Week 51: Perseverance and Enduring Hope

This week, our second "Deeper Dive" focuses on the intertwined themes of **Perseverance and Enduring Hope**, which serve as a powerful backbone throughout the General Epistles. These letters were written to believers facing various forms of pressure, persecution, false teaching, internal strife, and the daily grind of living a godly life in an ungodly world. In response, the authors consistently point their readers to the unwavering faithfulness of God and the ultimate triumph of Christ, providing the necessary motivation to stand firm.

Hebrews repeatedly urges readers not to "shrink back" but to "persevere" (Hebrews 10:39, 12:1), reminding them of the great cloud of witnesses and the ultimate prize set before them in Christ. James emphasizes patience in suffering and waiting for the Lord's coming (James 5:7-11), teaching that trials produce perseverance (James 1:2-4).

Peter, who himself experienced immense suffering for Christ, comforts believers with the promise of a "living hope" that endures through trials, refining their faith for future glory (1 Peter 1:3-9, 4:12-19). Even Jude, while warning against apostasy, calls believers to "keep yourselves in God's love as you wait for the mercy of our Lord Jesus Christ to bring you to eternal life" (Jude 21).

This collective emphasis highlights that the Christian journey is a marathon, not a sprint. It requires steadfastness, courage, and a deep-seated conviction that God is faithful to His promises. The General

Epistles equip believers with the perspective and encouragement needed to endure to the end, firmly fixed on their ultimate hope in Christ.

Devotional Thought: The Anchor of Hope in the Storm

Life often throws us into rough waters,, whether it's personal hardship, societal pressures, or spiritual attacks. In these moments, it's easy to feel adrift. The General Epistles offer us an essential lifeline: the **anchor of hope** that allows us to **persevere** through any storm.

This hope isn't a vague optimism; it's a certainty rooted in the character of God and the finished work and promised return of Jesus Christ. Peter tells us our inheritance is imperishable and kept in heaven (1 Peter 1:4). Hebrews reminds us that Jesus is our High Priest, who sympathizes with our weaknesses, and we can approach His throne with confidence (Hebrews 4:14-16).

This week, as you reflect on the unwavering hope these letters provide, consider how this hope empowers you to persevere in your current challenges. What specific promises from God's Word serve as your anchor? How can you cultivate a deeper, more resilient hope that sustains you through difficulty and compels you to run the race with endurance?

Key Scriptures:

- **Hebrews 6:10-12:** Don't Be Sluggish, But Imitate Those Who Inherit Through Faith and Patience

- **Hebrews 10:35-39:** Do Not Throw Away Your Confidence; You Need Endurance

- **Hebrews 12:1-3:** Run the Race with Perseverance, Fixing Our Eyes on Jesus

- **James 1:2-4:** Trials Produce Perseverance

- **James 5:7-11:** Be Patient Until the Lord's Coming; Examples of Endurance

- **1 Peter 1:3-9:** A Living Hope Through Resurrection, Tested by Suffering

- **1 Peter 4:12-19:** Suffering for Christ's Name and Future Glory

- **1 Peter 5:6-11:** Humble Yourselves, Cast Your Anxieties, God Will Restore

- **2 Peter 3:8-14:** The Certainty of Christ's Coming and Living in Light of It

- **Jude 20-21:** Building Yourselves Up in the Faith, Keeping in God's Love, Waiting for Mercy

Reflection Questions:

1. How do the authors of Hebrews and James connect the idea of trials with the development of perseverance? What is the intended outcome?

2. What does it mean to "run with endurance" as described in Hebrews 12:1? How is looking to Jesus central to this endurance?

3. Peter repeatedly links suffering with future glory (e.g., 1 Peter 1:6-7, 4:13). How does this perspective change how we view present difficulties?

4. In what ways does the **certainty of Christ's return** (as seen in James 5 and 2 Peter 3) serve as a motivation for patience and holy living?

5. Reflect on a time when your hope in God helped you persevere through a difficult situation. What lessons did you learn about God's faithfulness and your own capacity for endurance?

Week 51 Workbook

Date: _____

Key Takeaways from Devotional Thought:

_____

_____

_____

_____

_____

Insights from this week's Bible study:

_____

_____

_____

_____

_____

Devotional Reflection: What Biblical insights on perseverance did you gain from God's Word this week?

_____

_____

_____

_____

_____

_____

_____

_____

_____

_____

Part 10: Revelation – The End and Beginning

After journeying through the Law, History, Poetry, Prophets, Gospels, Acts, Paul's Epistles, and the General Epistles, we arrive at the final book of the Bible: **Revelation**. This dramatic and symbolic book serves as God's culminating word to humanity, pulling back the curtain to reveal ultimate triumph, justice, and the glorious future of God's people.

Week 52: Revelation – God's Triumphant End and New Beginning

This week marks the culmination of our year-long journey through the Bible as we delve into the book of **Revelation**. Penned by the Apostle John during his exile on the island of Patmos, Revelation is a prophetic vision revealing "what must soon take place" (Revelation 1:1). It offers a profound message of hope, warning, and assurance to believers across the ages.

Revelation primarily serves two critical purposes:

1. **To warn and challenge believers:** It unmasks the true nature of evil, exposing the spiritual forces at work behind earthly persecution and deception. It calls for faithfulness and perseverance, even unto death, urging believers not to compromise with the corrupting influences of the world.

2. **To offer comfort and hope:** Amidst vivid descriptions of judgment and spiritual warfare, the overriding message is one of ultimate victory. It reveals Jesus Christ as the triumphant Lamb, the King of kings and Lord of lords, who will ultimately conquer all evil, establish His eternal kingdom, and dwell with His people in a new heaven and new earth.

While rich in symbolism and apocalyptic imagery, Revelation is fundamentally about God's sovereign control over history, the certain defeat of evil, and the glorious consummation of His plan of redemption. It assures us that, no matter the present chaos, God has the final word, and His faithful followers will share in His eternal glory.

Devotional Thought: Looking Up, Living Out

Revelation invites us to lift our gaze beyond our immediate circumstances and fix it on the grand narrative of God's redemptive plan. It reminds us that our story is interwoven with His, culminating in Christ's triumphant return and the establishment of perfect justice and peace. This future hope is not meant to inspire escapism, but courageous endurance and faithful living in the present. Knowing that evil will not have the last word, and that ultimate victory belongs to Christ, empowers us to stand firm against temptation, speak truth in a deceptive world, and live holy lives.

This week, as you reflect on the majestic visions of Revelation, how does the assurance of God's ultimate victory and the promise of a new heaven and new earth impact your daily life? How can this profound hope empower you to live with greater courage, faithfulness, and anticipation for Christ's return?

Key Scriptures:

- **Revelation 1:4-8:** The Vision of the Risen Christ
- **Revelation 2-3:** Messages to the Seven Churches (Call to Repentance and Perseverance)
- **Revelation 4-5:** The Throne Room of God and the Lamb Who Was Slain
- **Revelation 7:9-17:** The Redeemed Multitude Before the Throne
- **Revelation 12:** The Woman, the Dragon, and Spiritual Warfare
- **Revelation 19:11-16:** Christ the Victorious King
- **Revelation 20:1-6:** The Millennial Reign
- **Revelation 20:11-15:** The Great White Throne Judgment
- **Revelation 21:1-8:** The New Heaven and New Earth
- **Revelation 22:1-5:** The River of Life and the Tree of Life
- **Revelation 22:12-21:** Final Warnings and Invitations

Reflection Questions:

1. What is the main message of the letters to the seven churches in Revelation 2-3? How are these messages relevant to churches and individual believers today?

2. Describe the central vision of God's throne room in Revelation 4-5. What does this reveal about God's character and the role of the Lamb (Jesus)?

3. Despite intense imagery of suffering and judgment, Revelation is ultimately a book of hope. What specific passages or themes give you the greatest hope and assurance?

4. How does the promise of a new heaven and new earth (Revelation 21-22) provide motivation for faithful living in the present?

5. What aspects of Revelation challenge or encourage you most concerning your perseverance in faith and your readiness for Christ's return?

Week 52 Workbook

Date: _____

Key Takeaways from Devotional Thought:

_____

_____

_____

_____

Insights from this week's Bible study:

_____

_____

_____

_____

Devotional Reflection: How did this week's study deepen your understanding of God's promises for a prosperous future?

_____

_____

_____

_____

_____

_____

_____

_____

Conclusion:
A Faith Confidently Lived

We have now journeyed through the entire canon of Scripture, from the foundational narratives of Genesis to the triumphant visions of Revelation. We've seen God's unfolding plan of redemption, the consistent nature of His character, the profound love revealed in Jesus Christ, and the practical implications of living as His people.

This systematic study wasn't merely an academic exercise; it was an invitation to **a faith confidently lived**. What does this mean?

It means understanding that our faith is **rooted in historical truth and divine revelation**. It's not a blind leap, but a reasoned trust in a God who has consistently revealed Himself through His Word and His Son.

It means living with **purpose and intentionality**, informed by God's commands and empowered by His Spirit. We've learned about practical godliness, justice, love for one another, and our call to be light in a dark world.

It means facing trials and suffering with **enduring hope**, knowing that God is sovereign, that our struggles refine us, and that our future with Christ is secure.

And finally, it means anticipating the future with **confidence**, knowing that Jesus Christ will return, that justice will prevail, and that a new heaven and new earth await those who belong to Him.

As you step forward from this 52-week journey, carry with you the rich truths you've encountered. Let the Word of God dwell richly within you, guiding your steps, transforming your heart, and empowering you to live a life that glorifies Him. This is not the end of your learning, but a powerful foundation upon which to continue growing in grace and in the knowledge of our Lord and Savior Jesus Christ.

Go now, and live a faith confidently lived, for the glory of God.

Check out another book in the series

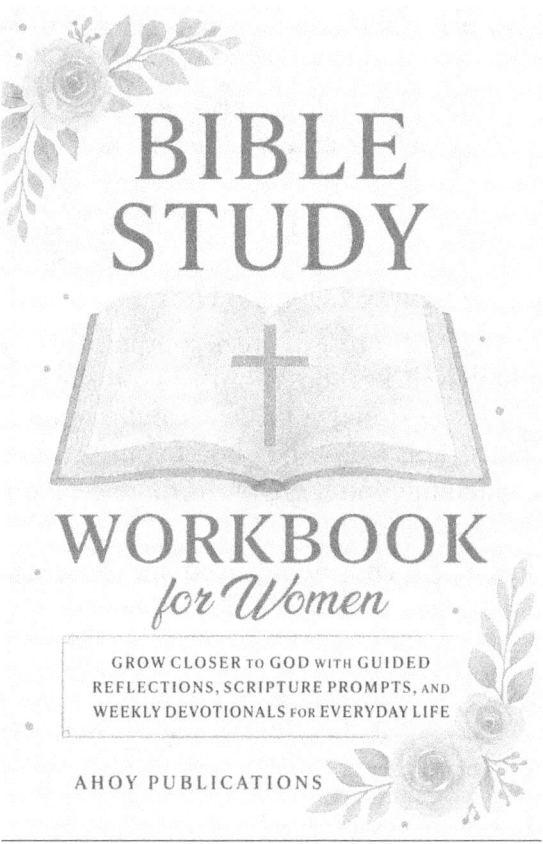

Welcome Aboard, Check Out This Limited-Time Free Bonus!

Ahoy, reader! Welcome to the Ahoy Publications family, and thanks for snagging a copy of this book! Since you've chosen to join us on this journey, we'd like to offer you something special.

Check out the link below for a FREE e-book filled with delightful facts about American History.

But that's not all - you'll also have access to our exclusive email list with even more free e-books and insider knowledge. Well, what are ye waiting for? Click the link below to join and set sail toward exciting adventures in American History.

Access your bonus here
https://ahoypublications.com/
Or, Scan the QR code!